Observing and Assessing for the Foundation Stage Profile

Vicky Hutchin

Hodder & Stoughton

A MEMBER OF THE HODDER HEADLINE GROUP

Also by Vicky Hutchin:

Tracking Significant Achievement in the Early Years

Right from the Start

Orders: please contact Bookpoint Ltd, 130 Milton Park, Abingdon, Oxon OX14 4SB. Telephone: (44) 01235 827720. Fax: (44) 01235 400454. Lines are open from 9.00 to 6.00, Monday to Saturday, with a 24-hour message answering service. You can also order through our website www.hodderheadline.co.uk.

British Library Cataloguing in Publication Data
A catalogue record for this title is available from the British Library

ISBN 0 340 81212 5

First published 2003
Impression number 10 9 8 7 6 5 4 3
Year 2009 2008 2007 2006 2005 2004

Papers used in this book are natural, renewable and recyclable products. They are made from wood grown in sustainable forests. The logging and manufacturing processes conform to the environmental regulations of the country of origin.

Cover photo from Sally and Richard Greenhill.
Typeset by Servis Filmsetting Ltd, Manchester.

Printed in Great Britain for Hodder & Stoughton Educational, a division of Hodder Headline, 338 Euston Road, London NW1 3BH, by Martins The Printers, Berwick on Tweed, England.

Contents

Acknowledgements

I wish to thank all the parents, children and foundation stage staff at Alleyns Junior School, Bond Primary School, the Dorothy Gardner Early Childhood Centre, Fircroft Primary School, Four Acres Primary School and Early Years Centre, Ridgeway Primary School, St Ann's Special School and Tunstall Nursery School. Thanks are also due to children, parents and staff at Sandhurst Infant and Nursery School and North Islington Nursery School for permission to use some observations.

Very special thanks are due to all those early years practitioners who work so tirelessly to do their best for the children in their care, and who also found the time to discuss their practice with me. In particular, thank you so much to Andrea Sully and team; Anna Skinner and team; Dilwen Roberts (for many discussions); Lesley Rampersad; Lisa Francis and Angela West; Liz de Keller and team; Myrtle Nixon (for her wonderful observations); Sarah Hosken; and Sue Hirscheimer. Last but not least, thank you, Billy, for all the support and understanding.

Vicky Hutchin

Introduction

The foundation stage begins when children are three years old (usually in a nursery setting or playgroup) and continues until the end of the school year in which they become five, when they are usually in a reception class. There is a distinct curriculum and approach to teaching, outlined in the *Curriculum Guidance for the Foundation Stage* (QCA, 2000), which places play in a central position. The **Foundation Stage Profile**, the new statutory assessment for the end of the reception year, has now been introduced to match this curriculum.

The foundation stage and the Foundation Stage Profile advocate that the assessment of young children should be based on observations. In many nursery schools and classes around the country this practice is already working effectively, celebrating children's achievements. The Profile now makes similar demands on reception teachers, and some are finding this quite a daunting prospect.

This book is for foundation stage (nursery and reception) teachers, headteachers, assessment coordinators, advisers and other practitioners – in fact, all those likely to be involved! It is a practical guide to the *processes of assessment* leading up to the Foundation Stage Profile at the end of the reception year. There are explanations of the processes involved and the principles underpinning this type of assessment. There are lots of examples of observations and guidance on how to observe; there are samples of children's achievements and case studies of practitioners who have set up their own effective assessment systems.

The book aims to answer the following questions:
- What are the requirements, expectations and underlying principles of the Foundation Stage Profile? How does this link with the expectations for the foundation stage itself?
- How should observations be carried out?
- What is good early years assessment practice and how can a manageable system be devised and coordinated across the foundation stage?

■   How can parents be involved?
■   Should children themselves be involved and if so, how?

Most of all, the book stresses how observing children learning and using the information gathered from this can be one of the most interesting and even exciting aspects of the teaching process. Rather than a chore, it can become a delight. And into the bargain, you will be fulfilling your statutory requirements!

How this book works

Chapter 1 describes the new Foundation Stage Profile and puts it into the context of recent developments in early years education.

Chapter 2 examines the role of assessment in learning and teaching and how this links closely to the principles of the foundation stage itself. Theories of learning and recent research are put into a practical context.

Chapter 3 considers some principles for formative assessment and how these need to be met in practice.

Chapter 4 gets down to the business of outlining in detail how to carry out observations and collect ongoing evidence of learning in early years classes in a manageable way.

Chapter 5 considers how to involve parents and the children themselves in the assessment process in a meaningful way.

Chapter 6 has case studies of practitioners and their classes in a range of schools, including a special school and an independent school, who have found great ways to incorporate observations into their daily practice. Some of them have developed their practice in the light of new work in the international context.

Chapter 7 examines the process of using assessment to inform planning – the heart of formative assessment *for* learning – as well as completing the Profile at the end of reception.

Chapter 8 discusses the implications for practice from implementing an observation-based assessment system. This is about setting up a real foundation stage learning environment.

Chapter 9 addresses some of the common questions which practitioners ask about early years assessment and the Profile itself.

Here is a taster of what this book is really about: young children learning! Calvin is 5 years of age, in a reception class. You will meet him later, if you read on . . .

Observation: 12.03 Calvin: Outside playing with paint rollers and water, mark-making. *'Do you know what? I just gave Scott my big roller 'cos he wanted to have a go and I'm sharing.'*

Areas of Learning: Personal, Social and Emotional Development

Assessment: Proud of his achievement in sharing scarce resources. Shows not only is he able to share and take turns, but also that it is an important thing to do.

The Foundation Stage Profile in perspective

1

The Foundation Stage came into being in 2000 with the publication of the *Curriculum Guidance for the Foundation Stage* (QCA, 2000). Officially a new 'key stage' in the English education system was born, based on six broad areas of learning, reflecting and promoting a vision of early education over which there has been a considerable degree of consensus by early years practitioners for many years. It was generally welcomed. One teacher's response to the Guidance was quite typical of many: *'Hooray! At last I have something I can share with parents which tells them what we do!'* In 2002 this became enshrined in law in England, as the first part of the national curriculum for older children.

The Foundation Stage Profile

The Foundation Stage Profile is the statutory assessment for all children at the end of their time in the foundation stage. This usually means children who are in the reception year. Increasingly schools are setting up Foundation Stage or Early Years Units, amalgamating nursery and reception classes into one unit, but some children, whose birthdays are later in the school year, may miss out altogether on what is called the 'reception class'. But whatever the organisation of class groupings, the statutory assessment is to be carried out on all children who are in their final term of the Foundation Stage. This includes many children who are in private and independent schools as well, if the school has opted into the nursery education grant scheme.

In lots of ways it is new and different from what has happened before – and from an educational perspective these changes are very encouraging. The Profile covers all six areas of learning of the foundation stage, and there are no tests and no set tasks. It is based entirely on teachers' own assessments, on the ongoing records and evidence collected from observations over the time that the child has been in the foundation stage. It is for *all* children, including children with special educational needs and children new to learning English as an additional language. It also involves what the children themselves think.

Amy Louise (in a reception class) said: 'I love maths. I've got a book at home with maths in it. Numbers and maths! I'm very good at it.'

Jaime, in a nursery school, said: 'I like the black scooter best, the fast one and I like playing with my friends.'

Vishal, in another nursery school, was asked what he liked doing best at his nursery. 'I like the cars, water and the sand. I like painting with a brush and some paint and the paper, but not every day.'

These types of comments from children are very much a part of the Foundation Stage Profile. Talking to children about their own learning helps practitioners to get on the inside of their thinking and understand what is important to them. As a result, our understanding of their development is deepened. In the reception year, the Foundation Stage Profile now makes this a part of the assessment process, through a child interview. This is a new and exciting development, giving children a voice in their own assessment, acknowledging their central role in assessment practice. The Profile also involves parents and incorporates their comments about their child's progress.

So far, so good: the Foundation Stage Profile is based on teachers' own records, involving all children and not only those who work with them, but those who know them best – their parents or carers. But what exactly is it, and what are teachers and other practitioners required to do? To a large extent, the success of the Profile depends on the successful implementation of the foundation stage itself, providing for all areas of learning in a child-centred way.

What are the requirements and expectations of the Foundation Stage Profile?

Every teacher who is responsible for children in their final term within the foundation stage must make assessments against the statements in each *scale* in the Foundation Stage Profile in June of that school year. This is statutory. Parents and children's comments should be added to the general picture before the final judgements are made. This summative assessment needs to be the basis for the statutory report to parents which every teacher has to make annually, and for the information passed on to the child's next teacher.

That deals with the statutory requirements. However, the most important question for practitioners is: what are the necessary assessment processes? What do we need to know and be able to do? How do we complete the Foundation Stage Profile?

How does the Profile work?

The Profile is very closely related to the foundation stage curriculum itself as set out in the *Curriculum Guidance for the Foundation Stage*. It covers all six areas of learning and the various aspects into which each of the areas of learning is divided. Without going into too much detail, this curriculum is broad and comprehensive. In all, there are 30 different aspects of learning. For each, there are three progressive bands of 'Stepping Stones' leading to Early Learning Goals, which it is assumed *'most children will achieve by the end of the Foundation Stage'*. Many of the Stepping Stones have several statements, and often one aspect of an area of learning has more than one early learning goal. This quantity alone shows the breadth of expected development and learning in the foundation stage.

The Foundation Stage Profile uses the Stepping Stones and Early Learning Goals but, whilst maintaining the breadth, the number of statements has been greatly reduced. It is 'a way of summing up' the accumulated observations and knowledge of the whole child, in relation to Stepping Stones and Early Learning Goals. As the *Foundation Stage Profile Handbook* states: *'The Early Learning Goals in the curriculum guidance were not devised as assessment criteria. The Foundation Stage Profile captures the Early Learning Goals as a set of thirteen scales, each of which has nine points.'*

Many of the points in the scales are not hierarchical (i.e. they do not go from less to more advanced skills) but focus on different aspects of development within the area of learning concerned.

The panel opposite just gives the bare bones of the system – and even then it still sounds very complex! But the great thing is that the Profile is based entirely on *formative* records, and in this respect it is quite different in philosophy, as well as the practicalities, from other statutory assessments in the English education system, to date.

All six areas of learning are included in the Profile. Thirteen scales have been devised within the six areas of learning:

Personal, Social and Emotional Development (PSED)

- Dispositions & attitudes (DA)
- Social development (SD)
- Emotional development (ED)

Communication, Language and Literacy (CLL)

- Language for communication and thinking (LCT)
- Linking sounds & letters (LSL)
- Reading (R)
- Writing (W)

Mathematical Development (MD)

- Number as labels & for counting (NLC)
- Calculating (C)
- Shape, space & measures (SSM)

Knowledge and Understanding of the World (KUW)
Physical Development (PD)
Creative Development (CD)

Each assessment scale has nine points. The first three points, based on the Stepping Stones, describe children who are progressing towards the Early Learning Goals. The next points, 4–8, relate to the Early Learning Goals, and the final point (9) describes a child who is working beyond the level of the Early Learning Goals. In order to be assessed at point 9, all of points 1–8 in the scale must have been achieved.

How are the assessments to be made?

Reception teachers are asked to make a 'best-fit' type of judgement against all of the statements in the profile, by looking at their accumulated evidence of learning, from observations and other sources, such as conversations with the parents and the child as well as nursery transfer records. This judgement *'should represent your assessment of the child's typical attainment'*.

There are 117 statements altogether and in most cases they are broad *summary* statements. One reception teacher said:

> *It isn't about the number of statements. It's about the records you keep. 117 statements are no problem, if you are carrying out observations, as most observations will tell you something about lots of the statements. You don't really need to spend much time making the final judgements.*

Children with English as an additional language can be assessed in their first language in all the scales. However, in *Communication, Language and Literacy* they can only be assessed as having achieved the first three points in the scales if their first language is used. The Foundation Stage Profile is intended to be inclusive for children with special educational needs, as it is a result of ongoing observations made during the normal daily teaching and learning context. The curriculum will have already been planned and adapted to suit the child's needs. However, where a particular scale is inappropriate to the child's level of development, these items can be left out, and alternative forms of assessment can be used.

Lesley, in a special school, feels positive about the impact of the Profile for children with special needs: *'It is important that children in our school have equality of opportunity with regard to the foundation stage and the Profile. We do recognise that some modifications to learning targets will be necessary, especially for children with severe or multiple and profound learning difficulties. The IEP (Individual Education Plan) targets will ensure that learning opportunities are appropriately challenging.'*

The Handbook and training materials for the Profile emphasise the need for good-quality ongoing assessment to inform teaching – or, in other words, formative assessment. The importance of this aspect of assessment is stressed throughout the documentation and the video material, although the only statutory purpose is summative, *assessment of learning,* at the end of the foundation stage.

How does it relate to previous forms of statutory assessment?

Before the introduction of the Foundation Stage Profile in 2003, the statutory assessment for reception was called Baseline Assessment. This took place in the first half-term of a child attending a maintained school in England, and was designed to show the child's level of attainment on *entry* to reception. There were many different baseline schemes (at one point over 90 schemes were registered), some using methodologies which were diametrically opposed. Some, for example, tested children in their first two weeks; others asked teachers to collect evidence through observations over six weeks. These were bound to result in very different outcomes. They were not linked into the Stepping Stones and Early Learning Goals, National Literacy or National Numeracy teaching objectives, and only three areas of learning were assessed: personal and social development, language and literacy, and mathematics.

With the introduction of the foundation stage it was time indeed for a change. The Foundation Stage Profile means that at last there is only one system for statutory assessment for this age group in England. There is no official requirement to collect baseline assessment information at the beginning of the reception year or in nursery.

The foundation stage in action

The Foundation Stage Profile means that assessment has officially caught up with the foundation stage Stepping Stones and Early Learning Goals. But, the foundation stage itself is a great deal more than the areas of learning, Stepping Stones and Early Learning Goals. It represents *a whole way of working*, starting from a clearly stated view of how children learn and what practitioners should be doing to support that learning. Here are some examples of children learning in a variety of situations – the sort of activities and learning experiences promoted in the *Curriculum Guidance for the Foundation Stage*.

In a nursery school:

Harris is sitting under the climbing A-frame outside. It is January and he and all the other children are dressed in thick coats and hats. Harris and another child have taken two small chairs under the A-frame. Harris is now retelling his favourite dinosaur story to another child and discussing the characters in the book. Harris often chooses books to look at and retell. His interest in dinosaurs is never far away.

Malak is in the home corner with some friends, playing at cooking. She is replaying the morning focused activity, which was making Chocolate Crispy Cakes. She used her own initiative in taking the lead role and remembers the whole cooking sequence in the correct order, pretending to melt the chocolate on the cooker, adding the rice crispies (from the empty box), putting the pretend mixture into the baking tray, then into the fridge.

In a reception class in a primary school:

Amy Louise, who we met earlier, is making a model with some 'reclaimed' materials (what we used to call junk modelling!). She says to a member of staff: 'Look what I've made!'

Practitioner: 'It's great. What is it?'

A.L.: 'It's an invention. Stars come out of here,' she says, pointing to the middle of the model.

Practitioner: 'How does it work?'

A.L.: 'You have to press this button here.'

In the first two observations, the children were involved in entirely self-chosen and self-initiated play. In the third, Amy Louise was involved in an activity that was adult-initiated –making models is one of the options they could choose to do during that session, although the 'workshop' area is always available for a range of making activities.

Harris's self-chosen activity is in line with two of his interests, about which he is passionate – one is favourite books and the other is dinosaurs. He is using his personal motivation to further his skills in retelling stories to an audience. Malak is using her newly acquired skills and knowledge, presented to her in a practical, motivating activity earlier in the day, in her play. In this way she is practising and rehearsing her new skills and knowledge, making them her own. Amy Louise is conveying her pleasure at her own creativity, showing self-confidence and pride, in a way that comes when children's own ideas are respected and valued. We will be finding out more about all three children later on.

If the success of the Foundation Stage Profile depends on successful implementation of the foundation stage itself, then it is important to look at the Curriculum Guidance in more detail. Given the right circumstances, what children can achieve, their creativity, ability to think and express their thinking can be quite remarkable. The foundation stage is all about extending, supporting and celebrating children's achievements and the Profile is about observing and assessing these. Fig 1.1 shows one such achievement: Jess, aged five and in a reception class, expressing in her own way her thoughts about growing up.

Fig 1.1 Jess – on growing up!

Learning, teaching and assessing in the foundation stage 2

In this chapter we will be looking at the foundation stage in more detail, exploring the links between learning, teaching and assessment.

The underpinning principles of the foundation stage

The principles set out at the beginning of the Curriculum Guidance for the Foundation Stage *'are drawn from and evident in, good and effective practice in early years settings'*. Many early years settings and schools were already signed up to these principles, even if not explicitly so. Seeing them prioritised in the document in this way was a validation of their philosophy and practice. The principles specify how effective practice is based on understanding how children learn, knowing the children well, and ensuring that every child's individual needs are met. Nearly all of the twelve principles have implications for planning and assessment. The following points are highlighted. Practitioners need to:

- ensure they make provision for children's learning that *supports and extends* their knowledge, skills, understanding and confidence;
- *build on* what children already know and can do, encouraging a positive attitude and disposition to learn;
- provide for children's *different starting points* and different levels of learning needs;
- provide relevant and appropriate 'content' that *matches the children's needs* (through activities planned by adults and those that the children plan or initiate themselves).

None of this can be done, of course, without finding out about each child first, making ongoing assessments based on observing the child in action, communicating with her or him and talking to those who know the child well. It is only through observing children and knowing them well that appropriate provision can be made which addresses both their learning styles and level of development. One principle is specifically about the need for observation: *'Practitioners must be able to observe and respond appropriately to children.'*

Knowing children well means knowing about their learning styles, interests, passions, knowing how they are in play, how they explore, and putting this information to use by planning in relation to it. It means knowing about the backgrounds, cultural heritage, abilities and needs and building on these to ensure *'all children feel included, secure and valued'*.

Assessing the processes of learning

In the foundation stage there is a focus on the *processes of learning*, not just on outcomes and many Early Learning Goals are about processes. This is also evident in some of the assessment statements in the Foundation Stage Profile scales. One scale is specifically about

---

Personal, Social and Emotional Development: Social Development

'Forms good relationships with adults and peers.'

Communication, Language and Literacy: Language for Communication & for Thinking

'Uses talk to organise, sequence and clarify thinking, ideas, feelings and events, exploring the meanings and sounds of new words.'

Knowledge and Understanding of the World

'Asks questions about why things happen and how things work. Looks closely at similarities and differences, patterns and change.'

Creative Development

'Explores colour, texture, shape, form and space in two and three dimensions.'

dispositions and attitudes, but in the other scales too there are many statements which describe learning processes rather than outcomes – see panel.

Learning and teaching in the foundation stage

There is a great deal of practical advice for practitioners in the *Curriculum Guidance for the Foundation Stage* and, significantly, in every section, **learning** comes before **teaching**: teaching is seen in the light of how children learn. This is very different from the type of educational theory which underpins the national curriculum, or the Literacy and Numeracy strategies, where the emphasis is on the teaching rather than learning. On the other hand, the Curriculum Guidance emphasises that what we know about how children learn *must* be used to inform the approach that is taken to teaching.

A principal phrase in the Curriculum Guidance is: *'play is a key way that children learn'*. The document states how children learn through playing and communicating. It points out how they learn from each other, through their senses, through being active, physically experiencing their environment and what they encounter. It highlights how children need time to explore, the importance of feeling emotionally secure, making connections between what they already know and what they are finding out, and the importance of creativity and imagination. Children learn through *'having an idea and testing it out; as a result they may adapt the model they are making, try out a different way of dancing, take a new direction in their imaginative play or ask you a probing question'*.

The principles in the Curriculum Guidance come from well-established theories and research about children's learning and teaching. There is only a brief outline in the Guidance of how children learn, but understanding more about what underpins the foundation stage can inform what we do with the children. And, if we are to make assessments on children's learning, the first task in assessing learning is to make sure it really is going on!

What do we know about how children learn?

The importance of social relationships and play to learning

Play in the reception class has been very important to **Srikajan**'s learning. Srikajan, whose first language is Tamil, was new to learning English when he began school in September. Later on in the year the role play area was set up as a library for the school's book week and Srikajan spent a lot of time there, developing skills in all areas of learning. In play, he was able to explain to an adult how to be a librarian, showing confidence and skills in English, literacy and numeracy.

'You get that book, look, and then there's some numbers in it. You take the hat and the glasses and look at the number – it's number 2! Now you do that!' (takes stamp pad and stamps the book). Writes some other numbers he knows and reads them back to adult.

In this example, Srikajan is able to demonstrate both what he knows about numbers and libraries and also what he is learning through play. Our understanding of children's learning owes a great deal to the work of the Russian psychologist, Lev Vygotsky, writing in the 1920s, but as influential today as ever. He considered that along with language and communication, play, exploration and social interaction are vital ingredients of the learning process and development of thinking.

Vygotsky (1978) believed that in play children operate at their highest level, *'beyond his average age, above his daily behaviour; in play it is as though he were a head taller than himself'*. The central role of play to learning is now very well established. Play gives opportunities for self-expression and creativity, opportunities to collaborate and negotiate with others, to rehearse and practise newly acquired skills as well as try out some not yet fully acquired, in a safe non-threatening environment.

Vygotsky also emphasised the key role adults fulfil in supporting children's learning. To make a difference, it needs to occur in the right way at the right time. Learning happens when the child is in what Vygotsky called the *zone of proximal development*, described by Wood (1998) as *'the gap between what the child is able to do alone and what he can achieve with help from one more knowledgeable and skilled than himself.'* With the right sort of help and support, the child is ready to take a tiny step in development or even a leap forward. Here is an example.

> **Ibrahim**, whose first language is Urdu and is at an early stage in communicating in English, told his teacher the storyline of his play: *'Aeroplane stuck, helicopter coming – it's a police one.'* His teacher confirmed what he said, at the same time modelling the language for him: *'Oh I see, the aeroplane got stuck and the helicopter is coming.'* Later Ibrahim was able to tell his story to the whole class and in so doing used a more correct grammatical structure because the support he had received during his play was at the right level at the right moment. Ibrahim said: *'The aeroplane got stuck. The helicopter coming.'*

The meaning of intelligence

In recent years we have discovered a great deal about how the brain actually functions and this is changing our view of how young children's thinking develops. It has been shown that the brain develops through making connections or developing 'new wiring', as a result of social relationships, communicating with others, exploring and relating to physical surroundings. Children learn a great deal from their environment and if this is rich and stimulating, and full of interesting things to explore, do and look at, then this will develop their ability to think. This has many important implications for teaching.

Similarly, changing views on the nature of intelligence are beginning to influence our understanding about children and learning. For instance, Howard Gardner (1999) believes that intelligence is not just related to straightforward intellectual competence, but is composed of seven intelligences in different fields: interpersonal and intra-personal, spatial, musical, social, linguistic, and logical.

The work of Daniel Goleman (1996) highlights the importance of *emotional intelligence* – having the necessary emotional strength and resilience to cope with life's stresses and strains. Making and maintaining meaningful relationships, coping with one's own and others' feelings, developing confidence and independence are all aspects of emotional intelligence. Goleman showed that children's success in school is more closely linked to emotional factors such as being self-assured and knowing how to behave than to actual IQ.

The concept of involvement

In Belgium, Ferre Laevers and his team have been researching the nature of learning in young children for the last twenty years or more. He believes that when children are deeply involved in what they are doing, significant, deep-level learning is taking place. Laevers has highlighted two key aspects of learning: *emotional wellbeing* and the concept of *involvement*. Involvement is related to children's innate 'exploratory drive, motivation and dispositions'. In the example, Abedalamir is intensively involved in learning.

Abedalimir became deeply involved in play with a tricycle, solving a tricky problem. First he attempted to fix some dough onto it. To solve the problem he told his friend: *'Get some Sellotape!'* The dough fell on the ground, but he turned his mind to another similar 'fixing' problem: he spotted a cart nearby, so he decided to tape this to the tricycle; he tried to ride the extended vehicle. He then organised other children to sit on the trailer and he pushed and pulled until he managed to move them both. Throughout, Abedalimir remained deeply involved, solving problems and investigating weight, joining strength, and his own strength in the process. He was able to take the lead, motivating other children to join him.

Fig 2.1 Abedalimir's tricycle and trailer

This is how Laevers (2002) describes the concept of involvement:

> *When children are concentrated and focused, interested, motivated, fascinated, mentally active, fully experiencing sensations and meanings, enjoying the satisfaction of the exploratory drive, operating at the very limits of their capabilities, we know that deep-level learning is taking place. If deep-level learning is taking place, a person is operating at the limits of their "zone of proximal development".*

It is deep-level learning in young children which will have a lasting effect, and it is therefore vital that early years education ensures this kind of learning is taking place. Laevers believes that practitioners can either enhance or impede children's learning. Increasing the levels of wellbeing and involvement will enhance learning. Both wellbeing and involvement can be observed in children and Laevers has devised systems of indicators of deep-level learning and also emotional wellbeing. This has become a powerful evaluation tool for early childhood settings and schools. The *Effective Early Learning Programme* (Pascal, Bertram *et al.*), well known to many in Britain and abroad as a way of evaluating quality in early years settings, uses some of Laevers' evaluation methods in its programme.

This is just a very brief look at some theories about learning which have had an effect on foundation stage practice in England. What is happening in other parts of the world is also having a deep impact on early years practitioners here.

An international perspective

The national early years curriculum in New Zealand, *Te Whariki* (1996), has met with much attention and approval in the early years community in Britain. The view that children learn through exploration, social relationships and play, in a context which supports the child's emotional wellbeing and allows emotional intelligence to grow is much more in evidence in *Te Whariki* than it is in the Curriculum Guidance for the Foundation Stage. As Margaret Carr (2001), a co-director on the curriculum development team in New Zealand, says: *'While skills and knowledge matter a great deal, they will be fragile indeed if institutional arrangements in classrooms and early childhood settings do not embed them in motivating circumstances. . . .'*

The influences from New Zealand are evident in much of the already well-established early years good practice in Britain, as we will see in some of the case studies in Chapter 6.

The Reggio Emilia approach

For the past twenty years or so early years practitioners, researchers and specialists have become increasingly interested in an innovative approach to early education developed in the town of Reggio Emilia in northern Italy. Outcomes for the children are exceptional, particularly in terms of their dispositions, confidence, social development, creativity and general cognitive development.

An important aspect of the Reggio Emilia approach is the way that children's interests – what motivates them – are built on through investigative projects where children's own ideas lead the investigations. Children are listened to and their thoughts are taken seriously – their creativity forms the core of the curriculum. Loris Malaguzzi, founder of the Reggio approach, used the now famous phrase *'the hundred languages of children'* to describe the many ways in which they represent and communicate their thoughts and feelings. The emphasis is on communication and discussion, creativity, exploration and creative expression. Through documentation which the staff display, the children's thoughts, ideas and creativity are captured.

Louise Boyd Cadwell (1997), an American teacher who spent a year working in the Reggio pre-schools, has written about her experiences there. She believes that underlying the success of the Reggio approach is the way adults perceive children. They are seen as capable, full of potential, curiosity and interest, they are part of a social network relating to others and part of a community. The teacher is seen as 'partner, nurturer and guide' as well as researcher, and the environment itself is also seen as a 'teacher'. Children and practitioners are given time to think and develop their ideas, unpressurised by a formal adult-led curriculum.

As we will see later on, the Reggio ways of working, nurturing children's creativity and taking their interests as the focal point of teaching is having a profound effect in some settings and schools across the country. It is influencing their pedagogy as well as assessment processes, planning and the way learning is documented and displayed – as in Figure 2.2.

❝ *This project came about because a bird table had been made for us and we talked about how to encourage the birds to come and use it, so children first made things for the birds, then some decided to write letters to them.* ❞

A Group Story

Children: Tyler, Katland, Nicholas, Bradley Date: 11th March		**A LEARNING STORY**
Belonging	TAKING AN INTEREST	The children had been excited by the arrival of a bird table in the nursery garden. They were asked if there was anything else they'd like to do for the birds. This inspired many ideas including, a 'surfing thing', 'a slide', and a 'bed for the birds'. We planned for the children to use wood to construct their toys for the birds and when completed, we put them ceremoniously out for the birds to enjoy. It was at this point that some of the children suggested they should leave letters for the birds, along with the toys! The children excitedly dictated their ideas and wrote their letters. They then pinned their letters to the tree.
Well-being	BEING INVOLVED	
Exploration	PERSISTING WITH DIFFICULTY	
Communication	EXPRESSING AN IDEA OR FEELING	
Contribution	TAKING RESPONSIBILITY	
Short-term review *Children demonstrated that they are motivated and excited about learning; able to discuss their work and make simple designs; handle tools safely; demonstrate curiosity and concentration; beginning to understand some purposes of writing.*	**What next?** Engage children in large scale sculpture of a bird, looking at wings and feathers. Investigate flight using paper aeroplane, seeds, kites, etc. Collect a tally of number of birds at bird table, observational drawings of feathers and birds.	

Fig 2.2 Birds learning story

Teaching in the foundation stage

Returning to England, the *Curriculum Guidance for the Foundation Stage* (2000) provides advice on what practitioners need to do to ensure children are motivated, interested, maintain positive dispositions and attitudes, a high level of involvement and emotional wellbeing. There is also an emphasis on play, and one aspect of teaching is seen as involvement in play.

> *Teaching has many aspects, including planning and creating a learning environment, organising time and material resources, interacting, questioning, responding to questions, working with and observing children, assessing and recording children's progress and sharing knowledge gained with other practitioners and parents.*

In this definition there is little reference to direct 'teaching', such as following the adult's instructions. This is quite different from the methodology prioritised, for example, in the National Literacy Strategy, where direction and demonstration come to the fore as teaching methods. The examples given for directed teaching in the Curriculum Guidance are, interestingly, for specific physical skills such as using scissors and staplers. Such teaching, it specifies, is based on being sensitive and knowing the child well enough to judge whether she/he is ready to be taught the skill.

The *Effective Provision of Pre-school Education* (EPPE) research project, a longitudinal research project commissioned and funded by the DfES in 1997 (the first project of its kind in Britain), has produced some important evidence about what types of early years settings are most effective. An offshoot from the main project, entitled *Researching Effective Pedagogy in the Early Years* (REPEY), examined the types of 'pedagogy' used in the settings which achieved the highest levels of attainment for children in the EPPE project. Siraj-Blatchford, Sylva *et al.* (2002) have used the term *pedagogy* as a more inclusive term than *teaching*, more relevant to the foundation stage, highlighting the role of interaction between adult and child, the effect of the learning environment, routines of the day and relationships with families, all of which impact on how the child is enabled to learn.

Their findings show that effective pedagogy means:

- episodes of sustained shared thinking between the adult and child, with both equally involved;
- practitioners extending interactions which the child has initiated;
- open-ended questioning;
- a strong relationship and understanding between parents and practitioners to support the child;
- an equal balance between teacher-led and child-initiated activities.

The researchers also noted a highly significant link between formative assessment and effective pedagogy.

Linking assessment to what is important in learning

The Foundation Stage Guidance makes much of the role of the practitioner as observer, pointing out the need for *'skilful and well-planned observations'* and using information obtained in this way in order to plan.

A teacher in a reception class, relatively new to teaching in the foundation stage, explained how she felt about this:

> *I really value observing now in a way that I never did before. As a student you are asked to observe, but now I see how important it is. You see how individual children are and how they are learning over time. Now I know about the need to stand back and observe rather than intervene. You have to be very careful to make sure you are giving quality time when you do intervene. It is more like dropping something in – not talking too much – then standing back again.*

Chris Pascal and Tony Bertram are well known researchers in the early years field in the UK, in particular for the development of the *Effective Early Learning Programme* mentioned earlier, used in evaluating and developing the quality of early childhood provision in schools and other settings. They have identified, through summarising recent research, that there are *'three core elements of the effective learner: dispositions to learn; social competence and self-concept; and emotional wellbeing'* (Bertram and Pascal, 2002).

They make a strong plea that if research from many fields is telling us that it is these aspects of learning which have a lasting outcome for children, then these elements should form the 'foundations of assessment'. They point out that: *'We live in an audited society where what is measurable is seen as significant. We need to ensure that what we are measuring truly matters and that we are not simply focusing on those things that are easily measured.'*

The Foundation Stage Profile goes some way to fulfilling this entreaty. Many of the statements in the Profile are broad summary statements, and very few of them could be considered as easily measurable. They require the kind of ongoing evidence that can only be collected through observing children in action. This is one teacher's view:

> *The observations we make are very important. For the Foundation Stage Profile there are some things which you need a lot of evidence about and others that you do not need much for. For example, all those statements which are about the whole child – you probably need about 10 stickers (short observations on self-adhesive labels) for those and lots of examples of work.*

Looking at assessment: from principles to practice

3

Let us start this chapter with a typical example of everyday learning in an early years setting:

> The staff and some of the children (just 3 years old) noticed a large number of snails in the flowerbed. A transparent container was brought to put some snails into. Suddenly, several children crowded around, watching, touching or picking up the snails. Some children stayed for a considerable length of time and more snails were found. Of the ones who stayed the longest, each took a different approach to and different outcomes from the experience – it became personal, tailored to interests and developmental needs. Laura was keen to handle the snails; Ben was fascinated by the snails crawling on top of each other: *'They're all cuddling'*; Jack was fascinated by the difference in size and the number of snails in the container. Afterwards he decided to draw what he had observed saying: *'I've drawn big and little snails . . . 12 snails!'*

The evidence of learning from this observation is just the sort of information which helps practitioners to understand children as individuals, with individual interests and achievements.

6 *Whenever I think about children's differences, my sense of the excitement of teaching mounts. Without the uniqueness of each child, teaching would be a dull, repetitive exercise.* 9

This quote is from Vivian Gussin Paley (1990), perhaps one of the best observers of children in our time. Her inspirational books about young children in her kindergarten class in the USA tell us so much about the role of observation in the process of teaching in the early years. Every day for many years, she tape-recorded children at play and in conversation with her, creating stories, then listened to it later in order to understand the children better, so that she could ensure her teaching was responsive to their individual needs and interests.

Fig 3.1 *Jack's drawing of snails*

In many ways her process is akin to *assessment for learning*, the type of assessment which *informs* teaching. The significance of this type of assessment to effective teaching cannot be over-stated. How else can we ensure that children are learning to their full potential? On almost every page the Foundation Stage Guidance makes a point about the role of observation.

The Foundation Stage Profile promotes assessment *for* learning by assuming that ongoing records have been based on a system of observing, making assessments from observations and planning from this. This system should, if working effectively, support children's learning. But the Foundation Stage Profile itself is merely a summative assessment system, assessing children's achievements in relation to the foundation stage. It may tell us about a child's level of achievement at a point in time, but it does not help children's learning or teachers' teaching. As the Profile appears to *promote* one kind of assessment (formative), yet actually *is* another (summative), let us clarify what is meant by formative and summative assessment.

Summative assessment

Summative assessment provides a *summary* of the child's learning and development at a point in time. This is assessment *of*, rather than *for*, learning. It serves a different purpose to formative assessment. In nursery, it is likely to be used for transfer records and reports to parents; in reception, it is the Foundation Stage Profile. As one teacher put it with regard to the Foundation Stage Profile: *'The statements themselves are not helpful for my ongoing assessment. You lose the vitality of the observation.'*

Formative assessment

Formative assessment, on the other hand, is assessment *for* learning, which means assessment to *inform* planning. To get the planning right, formative assessment needs to be based on observations of the children in action, in their own self-chosen play as well as planned activities. This is at the heart of quality early years provision. An observation is likely to show information such as what motivated the child, who else was involved, why it happened and something about dispositions, as well as skills and understanding. If assessment is to be useful for planning, all this is important information.

How has formative assessment been used in the early years context?

Formative assessment based on observing young children has a very well established tradition in Britain, dating back to the nineteenth century. It has long been a part of high quality nursery practice, as well as finding its place in many early years qualification courses as a way of teaching about child development. But recently it has been brought into sharp focus again in primary and secondary education through the work of Black and Wiliam. They examined a wide range of studies on improving the quality of teaching across the education spectrum to university level. They noted the marked effect on the outcomes for students in all of the studies which involved improving formative assessment practice. They concluded that:

❛ *Assessment which is specifically designed to promote learning is the single most powerful tool we have for both raising standards and empowering lifelong learners.* ❜ (Assessment Reform Group, 1999)

The REPEY research (Siraj-Blatchford, Sylva *et al.*, 2002), mentioned in Chapter 2, has shown clearly that where formative assessment is effectively used in early years settings, the quality of learning is at its best:

❛ *The research shows that the more knowledge the adult has of the child, the better matched their support and the more effective the subsequent learning.* ❜

From every angle, research is showing us what we have known for a very long time – it is making use of *ongoing* assessment processes to feed into planning, day-to-day teaching and responding to the children that makes the difference. The processes necessary for the Foundation Stage Profile should help to ensure it is embedded right across the foundation stage, in every setting. In many nursery schools and classes and some reception classes, this kind of good practice has been going on for years. Here is an example:

A Learning Story

After mysterious 'it wasn't me' holes began appearing in the grass, we decided the children needed a specific area in which to dig. The children discussed where it should be and, once decided, the digging began. **B**: *'We're digging up the grass for the digging patch,'* said one child. The adult said: *'What are you looking for?'* **C**: *'Worms for sure'*, **E**: *'Worms – in that big hole.'*

The staff planned to ensure they could continue and introduced resources such as magnifying glasses and a tray to observe the worms in. **H**: *'I like worms. I'm looking through the magnifying glass. It gets bigger.'* **S**: (holding worms) *'Crawl, crawl, crawl, crawl.'*

The REPEY research has shown us that where outcomes for children are at their highest level, there is an equal balance between teacher-led and child-initiated activities such as play. If this is part and parcel of how children learn most effectively, then this kind of learning must be included in what is assessed. This would mean that 50% of what is assessed should be children in play and self-chosen activities. However, observing a child in play and self-initiated activities is likely to be even more important than in adult-led activities because, as Vygotsky has shown, it is these types of activities where children show their greatest competence.

How can formative assessment support teaching and learning?

The Assessment Reform Group have pointed to factors shown through research to improve levels of learning of children in primary and secondary schools:

■ giving children feedback on their learning;
■ adjusting teaching to take account of the results of assessment;
■ recognising the influence of assessment on the child's motivation and self-esteem;
■ involving children in their own self-assessment.

These are all important aspects of *assessment for learning*. In order to give feedback to children about their own learning and involve them in self-assessment, they need to be made aware of the expected learning and outcomes of any given activity. This assumes that teacher-directed activities are the norm, unlike the mix of provision which should be going on in the foundation stage. But a key statement hidden away in an appendix to the Training Notes for the Foundation Stage Profile, which were not widely distributed, points out that: *'Given the open-ended and play-based nature of many of the learning experiences that children encounter in the Foundation Stage, it may not always be appropriate to share learning objectives before they begin activities.'*

The authors clarify that children can still be involved in talking about their own intentions afterwards and invited to make their own self-assessment comments.

Making assessment for learning effective in the early years

So, what does effective assessment *for* learning look like in an early years context? Let us begin with what it *should* look like, by making a list of principles which both fit with the expectations of the Foundation Stage Profile and match with what the research is telling us about effective assessment for learning.

1 The starting point for assessment is the child, *NOT* a predetermined list of skills.

2   Observations and records show what the child *CAN* do – significant achievement – not what she/he *can't* do.

3   Staff observe children as part of their daily routine.

4   Children are observed in play and self-chosen activities as well as planned adult-directed activities.

5   Observations are analysed to highlight achievements, needs for further support and used for planning 'what next ?'

6   Parents' contributions to the assessment process are central.

7   Children are involved and encouraged to express their own view on their achievements.

These principles, summarised from *Right from the Start* (Hutchin,1999), can be used to check whether an assessment system is fulfilling its purpose. They are not new and are already well established practice in many early years settings. Interestingly, in 2001, the Assessment Reform Group published its own set of ten principles of assessment for learning which have many similarities. These include statements such as:

❛ *Assessment for learning . . . should focus on how students learn; . . . should be recognised as central to classroom practice; . . . should be regarded as a key professional skill for practitioners.* ❜

Each one of the principles for foundation stage assessment listed above has implications for what schools and practitioners in nursery settings and reception classes need to have in place. So let us now turn to examine these implications.

Implications for practice

Principle 1

The starting point for assessment is the child, *NOT* a predetermined list of skills against which a child is marked.

> *Implications: Observing children is the starting point for assessment in nursery and reception classes, not the Stepping Stones, Early Learning Goals, the Profile scale points or any other checklist.*

Since the introduction of the foundation stage, it has become increasingly common for practitioners to use the Stepping Stones and Early Learning Goals as both learning objectives in planning and as assessment statements. However, they were intended as *guidance* only. Children are all unique individuals, who learn in their own unique ways: although they may be similar to other children, they each deserve to have their achievements, interests, and learning styles taken seriously. What is a small step for one child is just as significant as a leap for another, yet a predetermined list of skills will not show these important personal developments and achievements. A predetermined list of skills using Stepping Stones, Early Learning Goals or the Foundation Stage Profile scale statements will not produce the kind of focused responsive teaching which is necessary to meet children's learning needs. They are not assessment *for* learning.

Making observations of children in play and self-chosen activities from the beginning of their time in the setting or class, and talking to parents about their child, will give key information about each child as an individual so that the right learning experiences are offered.

Principle 2

Observations and records show what the child *CAN* do – their significant achievements – not what they can't do.

> *Implications: Are records always written in a positive way and do they highlight achievements? Is this useful for planning purposes as it only records what the child has already achieved? How can we ensure learning needs are also highlighted without being negative? What about when there are behaviour issues?*

The importance of building positive dispositions to learning has been highlighted in the previous chapter. The Assessment Reform Group emphasise the importance of 'learner motivation', which can be so easily damaged when assessment is perceived as negative and unconstructive. Assessment needs to be not only collecting information about children's achievements – however small a step that achievement was – but also must help to boost confidence, motivation and self-esteem. The way in which the information is shared with children and parents is vital. We have no right to condemn a young child's learning by writing negative statements.

Sometimes I see comments in children's records such as *'poor language skills'* or *'can't relate to other children'*. These are not observations, but negative, judgemental statements. Such comments only tell us that the person writing them has dismissed the child as incapable in some way. Other comments, made about children in adult-led activities, such as *'refused to write'* or *'showed no interest'*, just show that the planning for the child was wrong, not that the child was wrong.

An observation describes an action, event or moment in time. If an aspect of a child's development is causing concern, then it is crucial to describe in detail what was seen. The judgement comes when analysing the observation, focusing on what the child *can* do as well as what she/he needs help with. In this way the onus is placed on the adults involved to provide support. It is important to remember that it is the adult who is in control, not the child.

When, for example, a conflict has been observed, it is important not to ignore it but record, as with any other observation. It is in the analysis that the need for further support should be highlighted.

Evidence (example or observation):

Danny making Duplo models on carpet with 5 others. Conflict ensued when he grabbed a piece of Duplo from another child. Conflict resolved when staff member intervened.

What does it tell us about this child's learning and development?

In a situation where a number of children are working with a limited amount of resources, Danny needs *support* to ask for what he wants and wait his turn.

Implications for planning:

- Organise construction provision so that children are encouraged to choose from the range of sets (and possibly limit numbers of children in the area?).
- Ensure a member of staff is deployed here daily for a week, to introduce new system of free choice and to support Danny in asking for what he wants and seeing the possibilities of using alternative resources.

Principle 3

Practitioners observe children as part of their daily routine.

> *Implications: How can observation become an integral part of the teaching process? How can we ensure the observations are useful and used for planning? What skills do practitioners require in order to observe?*

What do we mean by *observing*? The dictionary definition includes the notion not only of *watching* but also *taking note*, with an intention of doing something as a result. There is a strong element of *purposefulness* in this concept, and some interpretations of the word include the idea of scientific investigation. If observing is to be useful, it must be carried out skilfully.

The Assessment Reform Group stress that *'assessment for learning should be regarded as a key professional skill for practitioners'*. In the early years context, assessment for learning is a three-part process: observing, assessing and planning. This needs to become a habit, a core part of the role of any practitioner working with young children. The solution to success lies in knowing how to do it and how to incorporate it into daily practice.

So, what are observational skills? The most obvious are watching and taking note of what seems to be significant. This requires:
- a thorough understanding of child development and *how* children learn;
- a knowledge of a range of observation techniques, so that the most appropriate can be chosen for the occasion at hand;
- a general idea of what to look for;
- an ability to keep an open mind, so that the unexpected, which is so often very significant, can also be noted;
- ability to write meaningful notes quickly;
- skills in making an assessment from what has been observed.

This is the focus of the next chapter.

Principle 4

Children are observed 'in play, in self-initiated and self-chosen activities as well as planned adult-directed activities'.

> *Implications: Are practitioners looking at children's learning holistically, and valuing what children do, their attitudes and feelings about the full range of situations they engage in across the day?*

It is only through gathering evidence of learning in an eclectic way that we can get a true picture of a child's real achievements, whatever their age and stage in education. The Assessment Reform Group also believe that the full range of achievements for all learners must be considered. In the early years context, to gather a holistic picture of the learner, learning in a range of play situations needs to be observed. It is also important to include the child's perspective on their feelings about where and how they learn best. In this respect, informal conversations with children can give vital evidence to feed into planning.

Principle 5

Observations are analysed to highlight achievements and need for further support. They are used for planning 'what next?'

> *Implications: How can we link planning and assessment effectively when every child is an individual?*

This is the heart of assessment for learning and is frequently raised as a point for action in Ofsted inspections. The Ofsted handbook states: *'To what extent are plans for teaching based on assessments of what children already know? . . . Do assessments trigger further action?'* Using assessment information for planning is at the heart of good teaching, but with a class of 30, without a clear process for this, teaching becomes less responsive to children's actual needs. Many teachers in nursery classes with 'part-time' children can be responsible for a good deal more children. Chapter 7 explains how this can be done both daily and on a longer-term basis.

Principle 6

Parents' contributions to the assessment process are central.

> *Implications: How strong is partnership with parents and how involved are the parents in the class? Can they be involved in bringing in observations from home as well as participating in more formal discussions?*

Parents need to be the starting point of a child's record in nursery and reception, as they will contribute key information about their child's learning at home, interests and passions. This involvement with parents in the record-keeping process needs to continue. It is now an official part of the Foundation Stage Profile. Observations from parents can contribute to the all-round picture of development, especially with regard to dispositions and attitudes. In Chapter 5 we will look in detail at ways of involving parents.

Principle 7

Children are involved and encouraged to express their own views on their achievements.

> *Implications: Is assessment something which is done **to** or **with** the children in your school?*

Young children start out in life with an innate motivational impulse to explore, learn and make sense of the world. It is the child who learns: we cannot learn for her/him, although we can certainly try to help. But if assessment is something we perform *on* children rather than involve them *in*, then we miss the opportunity for them to be able to become reflective, celebrate their achievements and take some initiative in what else needs to be learnt or tackled.

We need to ensure that children have a voice in their own assessment and in planning the next steps in their learning – even at this young age. Ways of involving children in their own assessment, as well as involving their parents and carers, is the focus of Chapter 5.

Applying these principles across the foundation stage

In many nursery schools and classes these principles have been well established and incorporated into practice for years, but this has not been universal. Many reception teachers have felt under pressure to focus on the structured aspects of their teaching at the expense of child-initiated learning, implementing a timetable suitable for Key Stages 1 and 2, but not meeting the expectations of the foundation stage. In such situations, the day is divided up by playtimes outside, a long lunchtime and daily whole-school assemblies. These routines have taken precedence over implementing the mix of teaching styles recommended in the *Curriculum Guidance for the Foundation Stage*. Changes to practice may well be needed, before an effective early years assessment system can be set up.

The ongoing, formative assessment process, based on principles such as the ones described, needs to be the same across the foundation stage years. Obviously, it is easier to set up a continuous record-keeping system in schools with nursery and reception classes, than where children begin their schooling in the reception year. Even if the reception class is a mixed-age group of Reception, Year 1 and possibly Year 2, this kind of evidence of all-round learning is invaluable in gaining a full picture of achievements. Although the nature of play becomes more complex and involved as children grow, it remains central to learning and should not go unnoticed, as it is so important developmentally.

If there is no nursery class in the school, then it is likely that children will have been to another early years setting such as a maintained nursery school, private nursery or playgroup. LEA early years education teams usually encourage settings to pass their records on to the next school. This is often via the child's parents, providing an ideal focus for talking to parents about their child.

The next chapter will consider the practicalities of collecting a breadth of evidence for every child, from observations and samples in a practical, manageable way. There is no expectation that observations will go on all the time or that everything that children do has to be observed! Meeting the principles means seeing observation as an integral part of everyday practice. Observations are one kind of evidence of learning that needs to be collected. There is also a wealth of other evidence which helps to give the necessary breadth.

Assessment processes in action

4

In this chapter we will consider the practicalities of observing and collecting evidence of learning. To create a rounded picture of a child's achievements, as wide a range of evidence of learning as possible is needed. This will enable practitioners to know and understand the children better, so that the curriculum and teaching can be as responsive as possible. It will also ensure accurate summative assessments are made for all the children at the end of the foundation stage, using the Foundation Stage Profile.

Whatever the setting, the effectiveness of the assessment system rests not on the *quantity* of observations but on the *quality* and *significance* of the evidence gained. Most evidence of learning will come from observing during the course of the day and collecting samples. Over time, observations will need to be made in different learning contexts and at different times of day to cover the breadth of learning opportunities provided.

Different types of observations will result in different kinds of evidence. For example, a planned observation taking place at a particular time of day will give you something very different from an incidental observation where a staff member notices, in passing, something significant happening – yet both are important. Taken together, these will result in a rich source of evidence about learning. It will also make the assessment process much more interesting, as you deepen your understanding of the children's learning. But it is *what* you collect, not *how much*, which is important.

What are the key processes involved in assessment in the foundation stage?

Observations and samples need to be 'processed' in some way in order to analyse what learning is taking place. I recommend using the basic process suggested in *Right from the Start* (Hutchin, 1999):

> **Evidence (observation or example):**
>
> **Area(s) of learning addressed:**
>
> **Assessment:** what does this show about the child's learning and development?
>
> **Implications for planning:** what next?

Although the evidence itself may come in very different forms – for example, a photograph, drawing or observation – and the record-keeping format may differ from one setting to another (for example, observation diary, sample booklet, significant achievement folder), the *process of analysing* these and deciding on the implications for planning needs to remain the same. All the examples in this chapter follow this format.

Storing the ongoing records

There are lots of ways of storing the records and practitioners need to decide on the best way for their needs. However, it is worth considering the following points:

- Are they easily accessible to staff?
- Are they easily accessible to children or can they be easily shared with them?
- Can they be easily shared with parents?
- Do they show that you value each child as an individual and show respect for all-round achievements?

Keeping all the records for every child in the group or class in one class file does not make them easily accessible or easy to share. The best approach is to create an individual 'record of achievement', 'portfolio' or 'significant achievement folder' for every child. (We used to call these 'profiles'!) Some practitioners keep their collected samples accessible to the children in a portfolio and the observations elsewhere in a file. I think it is much better in terms of accessibility to staff and children if both can be kept together. Many settings and schools use an observation diary format, with blank spaces to stick Post-its or self-adhesive labels. Figure 4.1 shows a range of prepared observation formats.

Planned observation

Child's name:

Observation: Date: Time:

Observer:

Assessment: *What did you find out about child's learning? (What was significant for the child?)*

areas of learning? (What was significant for the child?)

PSED (DA; SD; ED)

CLL (LCT; LSL; R; W)

MD (NLC; C; SSM)

KUW

PD

CD

Child's comment

What next?

Observation format for participant observation

Observation notes:

Areas of learning covered (and aspect withi...

What does it tell you about this child's de...

Planning/what next?

Observation notes:

Areas of learning covered (and aspect

What does it tell you about this child

Planning/what next?

Observation notes:

Areas of learning covered (and as...

What does it tell you about this

Planning/what next?

Knowledge and Understanding of th...

Collect evidence about:

- developing interest in and curiosity about the phys...
  this;
- developing skills in observing, asking questions, ...
  and investigating, talking about what has been ob...
- developing an interest and enjoyment in making ...
  (wooden blocks, construction sets, reclaimed ma...
  joining and fixing
- developing an interest in and talking about how ...
- developing 'making' skills and moving towards p...
- developing interest in and awareness of the pas...
- interest in and awareness of the local environm...
- interest in and awareness of other parts of the ...
  gained through other sources

Date	Observation

Fig 4.1 Some observation formats

Collecting the evidence: observations

What to observe

Observations need to be carried out when children are involved in different types of activities:

- play and child-initiated activities, inside and outside;
- teacher/practitioner-led activities, inside and outside;
- activities that teacher/practitioners set up for children to experience which have been planned, but which children will be expected to carry out independently for most of the time, inside and outside.

Each of these types of learning activities and experiences provided for children during the normal day will need a different type of observation technique, depending partly on the practitioner's role within the activity – i.e. whether it is adult-led or child-initiated. The different types of observations are likely to be as follows:

Participant observations

- when adult is involved in play with the children;
- when adult is involved in planned practitioner-led activities.

Incidental observations (catch-as-you-cans)

- when you notice something significant that you are not involved in (either planned practitioner-led or child-initiated).

Conversations with children

- informal conversations and discussions which are noted down;
- 'interviewing' children about their own learning and interests.

Recordings

- photos of children carrying out a particular activity or involved in play, showing the learning process;
- video;
- audio-tape recordings of play or discussions.

Samples

- drawings, independent emergent writing, photos of models, art work, etc.

Planned 'focused' observations

- in which the observer deliberately stands back to observe and does not become involved.

Other observations too will help to give a fuller picture of the child, such as those carried out by parents at home. We will see some of these in Chapter 5.

What to write in an observation

For all types of evidence – whether observations, conversations with children or samples – the important thing is to write down in short, quick notes what seems to be significant for the child. Look out for things you don't already know, anything new, different or just not previously recorded – there is no need to write lengthy details about *everything* that happens during the observation. The best approach is to use self-adhesive labels, Post-its or prepared formats (see Figure 4.1), so that the observations can be stuck or slipped into the children's records under the various areas of learning. Make a note of the date and the area of learning, leaving enough room for the assessment. Include a brief note about the *context* too.

Including something which the child said is always very useful, as it helps you understand the child's thinking, and also gives you evidence of her/his use of language. Often non-verbal communication and gesture is equally important as verbal. Sharing what you noted down with the child afterwards can help to boost self-esteem and confidence. When observing play, try to include anything the child tells you about the play. A teacher in one of the case studies in Chapter 6 told me: *'The most useful things to write down are quotes of what the children have said, with something about the context, the background to the observation.'*

Making the assessments

After the observation has been made or sample collected, it is important to decide: what does this tell me about this child's learning? For many observations, it will be quite easy to do this at the time, once staff understand what to look for and get into the habit. Sometimes it may require a few moments' thinking time or a quick discussion at the end of the session. With experience, the process becomes quick and easy – in most cases – to do at the time the observation is made.

Whether assessing a child in play or a planned adult-led activity, you are making an assessment from what you observed. In **play** you are making an assessment on the developing skills, understanding or knowledge, as well as the dispositions and attitudes that the child is making use of. In a **planned activity** for which there is a clear learning intention, you will be assessing in relation to this. Highlight what the child can and did do. If the child did something not directly related to the learning intention which you feel is significant, the question to ask is why do you think the child did this and what skills were in evidence?

Implications for planning

Every observation or evidence is likely to have *some* implications for planning – in relation to the individual child, and on a broader level in relation to the setting, such as changing a routine or introducing something new. For the child, implications for planning will mean:
- What can we do to help extend this child's skills or understanding in relation to what has been observed?
- What activities, learning opportunities or resources should we provide?
- How will staff be involved?

For the setting and staff, implications for planning might be:
- What do we need to change or develop to build on this child's interests?
- How can we ensure all children can access the learning opportunities we provide?

Let us now consider the different types of observations (page 39), and the practical implications of collecting them.

PARTICIPANT OBSERVATIONS

Participant observations are ones in which practitioners are fully involved in working with the children whilst they are observing them. This can include observations of children and adults together involved in play or child-initiated activities, as well as planned adult-led activities. Although being involved in an adult-led activity is very different from being involved in play, both require the same participant observation technique.

Participating in play outside and inside

Examples here include role play, imaginative play, construction play, water or sand play or any other purposeful play or child-initiated learning experiences.

Organising the observations

All staff need to get into the habit of noting down things as they work. If deeply involved in the play, write down what was significant immediately afterwards. So long as you are not interrupting the children's play, tell the child what you are writing, as she/he may add some comments for you!

What to look for

Any aspect of any area of learning could be significant, but the questions and areas of learning listed opposite may be particularly relevant. There is no expectation that practitioners will look for *all* of these!

EXAMPLES

In the Nursery

Observation: 6/02. **Malak** (new to learning English) playing with dough in the home corner alone, 2 more children come in and ask for dough and M divides it between them. *'I cook for tea. Look this is yours.'* Mostly play alongside each other but some collaborative moments.

Areas of Learning: Creative Development; Communication; Language and Literacy; Personal, Social and Emotional Development

Assessment: *CD*: able to share storyline with others: *CLL*: growing in confidence in use of English; able to describe own actions and give information to others in simple sentences in English; *PSED*: keen to share and involve others in play.

Planning: Continue adult support in play, to support further development of collaborative play and confidence in using English.

Assessing a child in play or child-initiated activities: some useful assessment questions

Personal, Social and Emotional Development

Dispositions and attitudes: who initiated the play/activity? Did the child introduce new ideas – if so, what? Did the child select or create any 'props' to use – if so, how? How involved was the child – did she/he show persistence/determination? How confident did the child seem?

Social development: was there any new evidence of building relationships, negotiating skills, sharing and cooperating with others? Was there evidence of respect for others and growing cultural awareness?

Emotional development: how did the child express feelings and/or respond to the feelings of others? Was there evidence of growing control over own behaviour – if so, how was this shown?

Communication, Language and Literacy

Communication and language (including other languages and signing): what type of language was in evidence? For example: talking about present, past or future events; sustaining a conversation with adult or child; using language to express imaginary or real ideas; using language to create or add to a storyline; using language to question or clarify thoughts.

Knowledge and Understanding of the World

Exploration and investigation: was there evidence of interest in exploring, observing, investigating, making predictions or giving explanations? Was there talk about how things work and, if so, what?

Physical Development

Physical Development: was there useful evidence about the child's developing fine or gross motor skills?

Creative Development

Imagination and creating a storyline for play: was there evidence of developing or sustaining a storyline, taking on a role or assigning roles to others, using props creatively?

Observation: 10/02. **Abedalamir** at construction table, picks up a picture of lego garage and asks adult to make it. Adult asks him to try to do it himself. He begins, using similar but not identical pieces. Finds car and places it in the garage. Spent over 20 mins at this activity.

Areas of Learning: Knowledge and Understanding of the World; Creative Development; Personal, Social and Emotional Development; Physical Development

Assessment: *KUW*: able to copy a design, build for a purpose and use the model for play (CD); *PD*: able to fix small Lego bricks without help; *PSED*: developing confidence in own ability; willing to have a go.

Planning: Encourage A. to make use of plans for other types of constructions; make use of maps, e.g. in bike play?

In Reception

Observation: 24/09 **Amy Louise** in home corner, taking a telephone message. Writes purposefully 1, 3, 11, 2, 10, 10. She reads all the numbers back correctly. Has written numerals 2 and 3 back to front.

Areas of Learning: Mathematical Development

Assessment: *MD*: Using numerals purposefully in play context; can write and read several numerals.

Planning: last obs. noted how she didn't appear to recognise numerals above 12, so continue to provide lots of meaningful purposes for using number through play and making use of displays to support.

Participating in planned small-group adult-directed activities, inside and outside

The *Foundation Stage Profile Handbook* has many useful examples of observations taken in these types of planned adult-directed activities in the 'case studies' chapter (Chapter 3). In fact, this is the only type of example in the Handbook.

Organising the observation

A planned adult-directed activity will have specific learning intentions on which to focus for at least some of the time during the activity. These should be shared with the children. You will already have an idea of what to look for in line with the learning intentions. But it is always important to keep an open mind: if what the child did is not related clearly to the learning intention, then what did the child do instead?

One reception teacher showed me how she created her labels for some adult-directed activities on the computer at the beginning of the day with the learning intention already on, so that all the adult had to do was add the observation. An additional label was used for anything else that happened. Many teachers choose to use lists of names of children to be involved, with the learning intention written at the top. The difficulty with this is that it is difficult to transfer into the child's individual record.

What to look for

Apart from how the child approached the activity in relation to the learning intention, there may be significant evidence about relationships with others, making connections with other learning or events and how the child communicates her/his understanding – or what the child did instead of the planned activity!

EXAMPLES

In the Nursery

> **Observation:** 10/02 **Donat** was able to throw the ball into the basket ball net successfully several times.
>
> **Areas of Learning:** Physical Development
>
> **Assessment:** *PD*: showed accurate judgement of distance and amount of force needed.
>
> **Planning:** Involve one or two others in throwing and catching games with Donat.

In Reception

Observation: 6/02 Showed **Paul** (in a special school) the 'Thomas' book, but he wasn't interested. Then showed him a tactile book: instantly interested and looked at each page for few seconds. Wanted to turn the pages from back to front of book. Really liked the furry tiger and kept going back to this page.

Areas of Learning: Communication, Language and Literacy

Assessment: Reading: showed a lot of interest in book of choice, decided which part he liked best.

Planning: Provide more tactile books.

Observation: 26/01 **Jess** outside planned focused activity: to observe closely how objects move.

Shrieked with delight as ball rolled down guttering and bounced off the end. Explored different ways of making ball bounce off: pushing it hard, letting it roll, dropping it onto the guttering, etc.

Areas of Learning: Knowledge and Understanding of the World; Personal, Social and Emotional Development

Assessment: *KUW*: able to devise own investigation and compare effect. *PSED*: shows independence and persistence.

Planning: Get her to talk at group time about what she did and what happened; ask her to set up investigation with another child.

Participating in large-group planned activities

There is a tendency not to observe children in large-group activities, although they are significant times of the day in both nursery and reception. This means a loss of some very valuable assessment information. With regard to the Early Learning Goals and the Foundation Stage Profile, there are certain expectations and scale points relating to children's participation in a variety of group situations in *Personal, Social and Emotional Development* and *Communication, Language and Literacy*. Children will often respond very differently in whole-group situations to how they are in small-group planned activities or self-chosen activities and play. So making observations on their responses, interests and how fully involved they are will be valuable. This is where implications for planning *for the setting* are particularly important: how engaged were the children and was the activity meeting their developmental needs?

Organising the observations

Before you start, decide which children you will be observing. In weekly planning, note down which sessions will be used for observing and which children will be observed. This serves as a good reminder in a busy day. If there are two staff, it will then be possible for one practitioner to observe for at least part of the time, whilst the other is leading the session. If the session is run single-handed, then reduce the number of children to be observed to one or two and write it up immediately after the session.

What to look for

You will probably be looking for the child's specific responses to the focus of the particular session and the learning intentions for this. Nevertheless, as with other observations of planned activities, be prepared to look out for other skills. Dispositions and attitudes, listening skills, talk, and ability to follow instructions will be particularly relevant.

EXAMPLES

In the Nursery

Observation: 10/01 **Billy** counted number of children at milk time to 9, accurately with 1:1 correspondence. Said: *'We need 9 milks then!'*

Areas of Learning: Mathematical Development

Assessment: *MD:* able to count with 1:1 correspondence to 9.

Planning: Offer opportunities to count beyond 9 in practical, purposeful events.

In Reception

> **Observation: Calvin** 19/11 Carpet time
>
> Teacher: *'I want to write "bag" – how can I do it?'*
>
> Calvin spoke up: *'You can use that'* he said pointing to alphabet chart. *'That one's got a 'b' at the beginning.'*
>
> **Areas of Learning:** Communication, Language and Literacy
>
> **Assessment:** *CLL*: Linking sounds and letters: able to make use of phonic knowledge of initial sound 'b'; knows where to find helpful resources and makes use of these.
>
> **Planning:** Encourage his independent use of chart in other writing activities – especially his play.

INCIDENTAL OBSERVATIONS

These are observations about things you notice that you were not involved in, almost in passing. I usually refer to these types of observations as 'catch-as-you-cans', as this describes exactly how they come about.

Organising the observations

This is when sticky labels, Post-its or notepads really come into their own – you need to have them with you at all times, at the ready, just in case! A great deal of useful evidence on every child in the class will be caught in this way. Practitioners will need to look out for significant things which can happen at any time of day – for example, the way one child helped another as they were washing their hands for lunch. Little things which catch your attention can be of particular significance in highlighting progress – often a small, but important step. Sometimes a child who is shy or new to English will rarely speak out in more formal situations or even when in play with adults, but will be much more communicative when in a small group of peers or with one other child.

What to look for

Use your existing knowledge about the child to decide whether what you have seen is something new and different. Sometimes, it may not be new learning that has been noticed, but significant because none of the staff have seen it before.

EXAMPLES

In the Nursery

Observation: 27/01 **Katland** stood by the fruit and milk trolley and pointed to the letter 's' in 'nursery' and said *'Look, S'*.

Areas of Learning: Communication, Language and Literacy; Personal, Social and Emotional Development

Assessment: *CLL:* able to recognise letter 's'; *PSED:* keen to share her knowledge with others.

Planning: Encourage her to find other letters she recognises around the nursery environment, and out of the usual planned activity contexts.

In Reception

Observation: 14/10 **Calvin** using props to retell story, 'Mr Gumpy's Motor Car', says to K: *'Put them all in the pile again.'* Then helps him do it and sits down, saying to K: *'When I read the story you can put the animals in the car.'*

Areas of Learning: Personal, Social and Emotional Development

Assessment: *PSED:* Able to work cooperatively with a partner, taking account of their need for support.

Planning: Continue to give C opportunities to support others.

CONVERSATIONS WITH CHILDREN

Informal conversations and discussions which are noted down

Some children are at ease conversing with adults, whilst for others it may take a change of situation such as going on an outing, or outside in the garden, to have the confidence to initiate a conversation with you. It is the children who are less verbally confident or competent, or perhaps just new to English, for whom recording such conversations bears most relevance. As with the incidental 'catch as you can' observations, these conversations are easily forgotten if not written down as soon as they happen.

Organising the observations

We know from research the importance of informal conversations to children's learning, so ensure that all team members are involved frequently in informal situations where they can chat with children.

Assessing an informal conversation with a child

- Did the child, practitioner or another child initiate the conversation?
- What type of language was used – e.g. explanations, descriptions of events, objects, places, etc, questions?
- How did the child express feelings and opinions?
- How confident was the child?
- How did the child show understanding and/or knowledge about the topic discussed?
- In children new to English or with language and communication difficulties, look for very small steps in development in these informal situations.
- How did the child use the language: e.g. using gesture, individual words, any new vocabulary, forming sentences?
- Note any new dispositions or attitudes (e.g. greater confidence and self-esteem, appropriateness of expression of feelings, developing awareness of cultures awareness, caring attitude, independence, perseverance, etc).

EXAMPLES

In the Nursery

Observation: 6/03 **Abedalamir:** Asked to listen to the tape his Mum has brought into nursery ('Going on a Bear Hunt' she has recorded in Arabic). He smiled shyly as he listened, turning the pages of the book. I asked him if he knew the word for snow in Arabic – he told me to ask E or M. I did and they said they didn't know. Then A said: *'Come here and I will tell you.'* Then whispered it in my ear. I asked him if I could tell E and M and he said yes. He was very pleased and told me *'Daddy said that.'*

Areas of Learning: Communication, Language and Literacy

Assessment: *CLL*: Able to translate single words from English to Arabic. Growing in confidence at using his bilingual skills.

Planning: Make sure he has more opportunities for listening to tapes in Arabic and opportunities to translate, supporting his developing confidence.

In Reception

> **Observation:** 29/02 **Calvin:** *'Do you know what? Me and my brother are going to see Nanny in hospital tonight . . . she ain't well. There's fishes in the pond outside and they have to eat food. But do you know one of them can't swim.'* Adult: *'It can't swim?'* *'No, cos it's stuck at the bottom.'*
>
> **Areas of Learning:** Communication, Language and Literacy; Knowledge and Understanding of the World
>
> **Assessment:** *CLL:* Able to describe events which are important to him, taking account of needs of listener. *KUW:* showing interest in nature, beginning to give reasons for why things might occur.
>
> **Planning:** Talk to him more about home events, thoughts and feelings.

RECORDINGS

These include photos, video and tape recordings which may be planned or unplanned. Photographs are an excellent way of recording learning processes, cutting out the need for lengthy descriptions of complex processes and so useful for sharing with the children and for sharing with the parents.

> **Always ensure you have explicit written permission from parents for photos and video, specifying how the photos will be used (in records and/or on displays in school or setting). Additional permission will need to be sought should the recording or photo be taken out of school (e.g. for training purposes).**

Organising the observations

Having a camera or digital camera to hand in the classroom is invaluable for all occasions, especially for recording play. But using video or tape recordings will need *time* to listen or watch the video and analyse it for evidence of learning.

Whatever form of recording is used, note the date (when the photo was taken or recording made) and some information about the context. It is also worth writing down anything the child said and any comments they make on seeing the photo, listening to the tape or watching the video.

What to look for

As with observations, you will be looking for significant developments, or celebrating achievements – especially the impermanent ones, such as block play, pattern making, large creative work, or physical play. But sometimes a photo is just a really good way of recording a typical event or learning process. Although it only takes a moment, a photo can substitute for the observation and can then be used as a prompt for analysing the learning that took place. Whenever possible, ask the child what they think is happening in the photo. This will add to your own assessment.

> **Context and background to an audio-tape recording**
>
> 13/1 **Malak** is at the tape-recorder listening to children recording their songs on tape. Tells the adult: *'You don't know my Arabic song.'* The adult asks if she wants to sing it. Malak eagerly takes microphone and sings in Arabic. She shows real pride when it is played back to her.
>
> **Areas of Learning:** Personal, Social and Emotional Development; Communication, Language and Literacy
>
> **Assessment:** *PSED, CLL*: M. can differentiate between the two languages she can speak and shows confidence in her bilingual skills.
>
> **Planning:** Play her song to others at group time and get her to teach us how to sing it!

Sarah, whose practice is one of the case studies in Chapter 6, demonstrates how much can be assessed from one photograph of a child deeply involved in play. Her format covers all areas of learning (see Figure 4.2).

Louis – 26/11/02		Age: 5.0

Personal, Social and Emotional Development
- Louis enjoys playing with his friends
- Louis cooperates well during play
- Louis is able to play for sustained periods at activities of his choice

Communication, Language and Literacy
- Louis is able to explain to the teacher what he is doing: "I am pouring it into the milk machine."
- Louis is able to communicate well with his peers during play

Mathematical Development
- Louis is able to use appropriate positional language as part of his play: 'into'
- Louis is developing a good sense of how much containers hold and when a container is full or empty

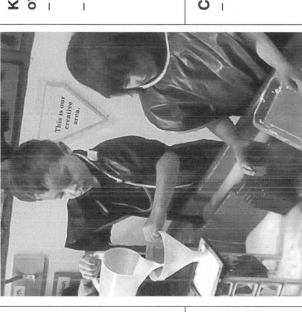

This is our creative area.

Knowledge and Understanding of the World
- Louis observes features of the environment.
- Here he talks about a milk machine

Physical Development
- Louis is able to pour liquid carefully through a funnel

Creative Development
- Louis is able to play in role with his friends as a 'milk worker'

Implications for Planning
- The children will be provided with different coloured water to encourage imaginative play
- Louis will be encouraged to develop this theme at the small world farm equipment
- We will continue to provide a wide variety of different sized plastic bottles to develop and encourage the use of further mathematical vocabulary

Fig 4.2 Louis' milk factory

SAMPLES

Together with incidental and participant observations, these will make up the majority of your evidence. Samples of evidence in the early years usually means significant drawings, mark-making emergent writing and writing, art work, and photos of models, construction, involvement in sand, water or other play. Remember that to make sense and be useful, each sample needs to undergo the same assessment process or analysis as for observations.

Reception teachers are increasingly moving towards the typical nursery practice where what children 'produce' – their drawing, mark-making and emergent writing – is likely to be on pieces of paper rather than exercise books, making the collection of these to go into an individual record much easier.

What to collect

Collecting samples will provide a good visual record of children's development over time. But because every child is different, it is most likely that what will be collected for one child will differ from another. You might want to ensure that there are some examples of mark-making or early writing and drawings, at least, collected in the final term of the nursery, as well as significant samples (such as photos), appropriate to the child. Then, in reception, the collection of writing and drawing in particular would be more routine, as well as other significant samples.

What to write

A quick note needs to be made, on any sample, of the date and the context, and whether the child chose to do it or it was part of a planned activity. Many teachers/practitioners feel that this should not be written on the child's work as this detracts from it. However, others feel that comments actually on the work can be more easily shared with children at the time. My own policy has always been to ask the child where I should write my comments, giving them a choice of where to position it (for example, on the back). Writing it at the time with the child present can be a useful self-assessment conversation starter, giving the child an opportunity to voice their own opinion.

EXAMPLES

In the Nursery

Donat: Name writing: January and again in March; **CLL**

Sample 1: painting his name;

Sample 2: I asked him to write his name for a model he had made –
I wrote his name for him and he said each letter as he watched me,
then wrote it himself. He was aware that it was incorrect and
wanted to repeat it. Really trying to get it right!

Fig 4.3 *Donat's name (January)*

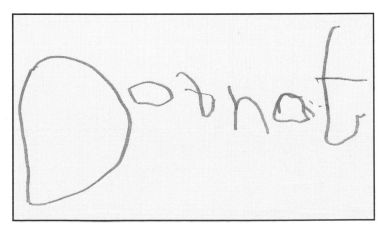

Fig 4.4 *Donat's name (March)*

Aaron: 19/11 'A wild jumping cat' **CD, KUW** Close attention to detail.

He drew this on a postcard he found in the writing area.

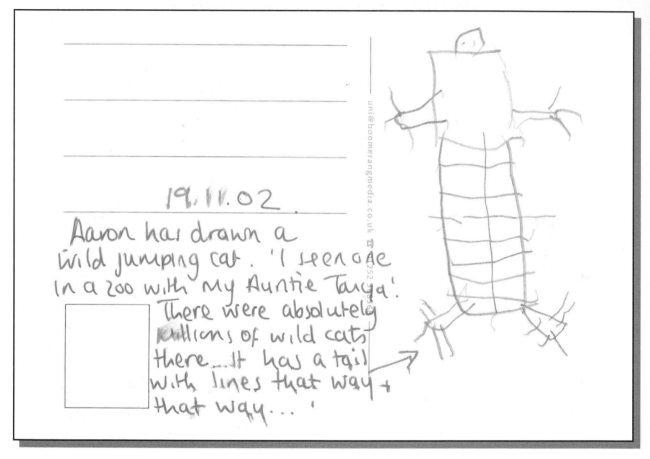

19.11.02.

Aaron has drawn a wild jumping cat. 'I seen one in a zoo with my Auntie Tanya! There were absolutely millions of wild cats there....It has a tail with lines that way + that way...'

uni@boomerangmedia.co.uk ☎ 0252

Fig 4.5 *Aaron's wild cat*

Julie: 26/11 Purposeful emergent writing; **CLL**
Wrote/drew menu in café to make an order for a salad.

Fig 4.6 *Julie's menu*

Malak: 12/03 In focused activity about size, Malak decided to make this picture on separate pieces of paper, then joined all the pieces together independently. **MD, KUW**

Fig 4.7 *Malak's 'bigger' and 'small'*

In Reception

Louisa: 6/03 Factual writing **CLL**

This was Louisa's first piece of factual writing. She wrote this after making a pot at school. She thought of and sequenced the stages herself.

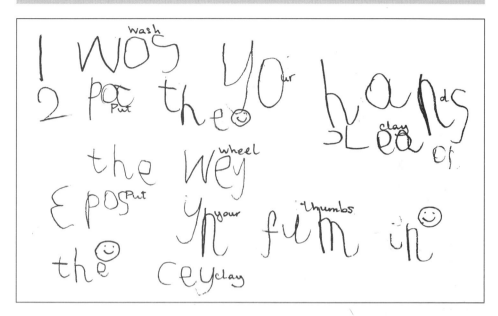

Fig 4.8 Louisa's first piece of factual writing

Fig 4.9 Paul, in a special school, drawing with chalks (24/03)

Meredith drew this story map and then retold the story as she pointed to the pictures. She used different voices for different characters and an evil, over-friendly voice for the wolf.

Fig 4.10 *Meredith's Little Red Riding Hood map (12/02)*

The majority of the record-keeping system will consist of participant observations, incidental catch-as-you-cans as well as samples and photographs. However, another important type of observation is the planned *'focused'* longer observation. The evidence from these is likely to be of a very different nature, showing a child at a particular time on a particular day. They often capture significant evidence which may have been missed through other types of observing.

PLANNED FOCUSED OBSERVATIONS

These observations give an insight into the child's choices, interests, relationships and how she/he functions generally, in a way that no other type of observation does. This is the *only* type of observation where the practitioner needs to stand back without being involved. It requires you to be fully involved in the job of observing, taking down as much relevant detail as possible.

Sometimes these observations are carried out for particular reasons – perhaps because there is not enough information about a child, or there is a particular concern. However, they provide an invaluable source of evidence for both nursery and reception, and practitioners should aim to do one of these on every child once per term. This should not be unmanageable, as they are *planned* observations and the time needed to do them is relatively short – just 4–5 minutes is usually enough.

Observing three children per week in this way will mean that in ten weeks the whole class of 30 could be observed. Some prefer to ensure that one is done every day, so that every child can be observed in 6 weeks – perhaps the second half of the autumn term, the middle six weeks in the spring term and early part of the summer term may suit reception teachers best.

Although some practitioners feel that this is the type of observation which is the hardest to manage during a busy school or nursery day, it *is* possible and many practitioners manage with no difficulties. The key to success is in ensuring that the children can work and play independently, effectively and purposefully without the need to intervene to help them access resources or sort out squabbles. A well-managed learning environment is essential – and as we all know, it does make a huge difference to children's success in learning.

Organising the observation

Many methods of observing are possible. Each will provide a different kind of picture for assessment purposes. Some methods are:

■ A five-minute continuous observation will show a continuous activity – it is best to do this on play or an independent activity, then you will also see what the child chooses to do.

■ Tracking observations, perhaps three times across the session at timed intervals, for about 3–5 minutes each time. This will show choices and pattern across the day.

■ Observe all children in one area of provision – e.g. role play, construction, etc. This could focus on particular types of skills or areas of learning.

Start by deciding what type of observation you will do, who will be carrying out the observations, when and for how long, and how you will choose which children to observe (e.g. each child on the class list in rotation?). Then add this information onto the weekly planning sheet and adjust your curriculum plans accordingly. Remember: this is a valuable aspect of your practice – not an add-on extra!

Record what the child does through writing notes, following the child for the duration of the observation. Note who the child relates to (if relevant) and record as much talk from the child as possible.

Making the assessment

Across all relevant areas of learning, make assessments of the child's skills, knowledge, understanding and attitudes, where these seem to show differences from what staff already know. What particular aspect of the activity seems to interest the child most? A useful way to make the assessment is to divide it up under different areas of learning, making a judgement under each area relevant. Using an observation format specifically designed for the purpose, as in the examples shown here in Figures 4.11 and 4.12, will help you analyse the observation.

The examples in this chapter were carried out by practitioners in a range of settings. Some of the children attended the settings which appear in the case studies in Chapter 6. All of the settings used a mix of observational methods in the way described here and made use of the evidence gathered to inform their planning. For some, these were shared daily in informal discussions; for others, a more formal meeting took place.

Although none of the teachers worked without any support from trained or untrained assistants, each had a different amount and arrangement for support. Some were in large teams, others in single classes. All of them saw observing, record-keeping and assessment as an integral and valuable part of their work with children.

Child's name: Joel (4.6 yrs)   **Date:** 18.11   **Time:** a.m

Observation context   Observer: *Rachel*
J with 2 other children (D and E) at water tray and has been involved in the play for about 15 mins.
4 minute observation
D: *'Waves coming'*, pours water from a jug
Joel: *'I'm going to make magic power'*, pours water from one jug to another
D then copies what J is doing.
Joel: *'Have to use these . . .'* (picking up play people from the tray) *'. . . to wash them. There's different ways to make magic power. The longest way is if you put sand in. I'm doing it the shortest way.'* Joel puts his hands in the jug. *'Now I've got magic power.'*
E: *'I'll drink it.'*
J: *'No, you can't, it will turn you into a pig!'*
Assessment: What did you find out about child's learning with regard to any of the following areas of learning? (What was significant for the child?)

Personal, Social and Emotional Development

High level of involvement in imaginative play with two others, took lead in developing the plot for the play

Communication, Language and Literacy

Able to describe his idea in detail and able to use superlative – longest and shortest. Interacts with another child appropriately to develop the play.

Mathematical Development

Makes use of mathematical language in everyday situation

Knowledge and Understanding of the World

Physical Development

Creative Development

Able to express and develop own fantasy play theme; able to involve others in this by taking leading role. Makes use of materials to develop an imaginative idea.

Child's comment

What next?

Talk to Joel about his play themes: especially the differences between long and short spells. Introduce more stories involving witches, spells and potions. Set up spell writing activities. Provide wider range of materials for Joel and others to make spells.

Fig 4.11 A planned observation

Child's name: Devano   **Date:** 3.03   **Time:** a.m

Observation: Observer: *Joan*
This was a longer more general observation, not specifically linked to IEP assessments or activities, in order to gather a fuller picture of child's achievements and interests
Devano is lying in soft play on his back and really enjoying being in here. Lots of vocalisations, even when I am outside with other children. He laughs as I tickle his tummy and tolerates S stroking his face. I help him to lie over the physio ball and he really laughs. Tries it both on his back and tummy. He stretches up on his arms when lying on his tummy to really look at S standing in front of him.
Assessment: What did you find out about child's learning with regard to any of the following areas of learning? (What was significant for the child?)

Personal, Social and Emotional Development

Expresses his enjoyment in a relaxed way and shows his interest in other children.

Communication, Language and Literacy

Making vocalisations and laughing to express his delight at the activities

Mathematical Development

Knowledge and Understanding of the World

Physical Development

Able to stretch up on his arms when lying on tummy to get a better view – motivated by interest in a friend

Creative Development

Child's comment

What next?

This activity is a regular occurrence, so we will continue to provide this for him . . .

Fig 4.12 *Another planned observation*

Involving children and parents 5

The most exciting element of the Foundation Stage Profile is that both parents and the children themselves are expected to have a voice. Although this is not actually a requirement within the statutory assessment, it is the first time that information from parents and children's own views have been formal expectations within a national compulsory assessment system in this country. In other year groups in school, there has been a growing emphasis on involving the pupils in their own assessment as an element of good practice, but no national expectation that it will happen.

The Foundation Stage Profile Scale Booklet contains two blank boxes in which to record discussions with parents – one intended for the beginning of the year and one for later on – and one box for a discussion with the child. These should take place *before* the final assessments are made. The emphasis is on *involving* parents in the assessment process rather than just informing them. This is the same for children – the discussion with the child is about listening to and valuing the child's views, not to tell them about the targets their teacher has set.

Why involve parents in the Profile?

In the section on teaching and learning in the *Curriculum Guidance for the Foundation Stage Guidance*, partnership with parents receives a high priority: *'Effective teaching requires working in partnership with parents because parents continue to have a prime teaching role with their children.'*

Practitioners and parents need to *'work together in an atmosphere of mutual respect'*. Embedding discussions with parents within the Foundation Stage Profile provides a supportive structure to turn this partnership, where it does not already exist, into a reality. The *Foundation Stage Profile Handbook* states: *'Practitioners should involve parents from the time when the children arrive in the setting . . . working with them to gain a shared picture of their children.'* They go on to consider the importance of the initial meeting with parents and ways in which the partnership can be continued.

Continuity between home and setting has always been a priority in early years settings. For many children this is the first time they have been in a group setting away from home. Ensuring that the settling-in period is carefully managed and supportive to child and parent is an important aspect of this. Long gone are the days when schools expected parents to leave their young children at the school gate – or even in the playground, lining up. A truly reciprocal relationship with parents, however, goes far beyond the settling-in or transition period. The early years classes in many schools and settings are at the forefront of developing new ways of promoting real two-way communication.

Sometimes teachers are sceptical about the information they gain from parents, as they feel parents see their child in such a different way from how the child appears at school. But this is precisely the point: to build a full picture of the child, an idea of what the child is doing and how she/he functions at home is invaluable. Parents and principle carers *do* know their child better than anyone else ever could!

For example, we met Harris in Chapter 1, reading a book about dinosaurs to his friend under the climbing frame outside. This is what his mother had said about him a few months before, together with some observations made in the nursery:

Parent conference comments:

27/1/02 *'Harris likes to play with dinosaurs, dragons, swords and animals. He loves looking at information books and having bed time stories read to him . . .'*

Other observations in nursery:

8/1/03 Harris completed a 24-piece dinosaur puzzle by matching the shapes to the picture.

19/3/03 Harris made a dinosaur from clay – it had a long neck and long tail. He put it to dry on some paper and I asked him to write his name. He wrote an 'H' then lots of oblong shapes; told me these were dinosaur eggs – *'big ones and small ones'*. Then pointed to other shapes he'd drawn and said these were footprints.

Ways to involve parents

The *Foundation Stage Profile Handbook* gives some helpful advice on involving parents in the assessment process. The video *Building the Foundation Stage Profile* also includes some useful footage of discussions between teachers and parents. There is a suggested format for a 'parent conference' and a shorter questionnaire for parents who cannot attend a meeting. The authors acknowledge the possible need for translators and interpreters, although this is not always easy to arrange in practice, particularly in settings where there are many different languages in one class.

Unfortunately the difference between the comprehensiveness of the 'parent conference prompts' and the simplicity of the 'parent questionnaire' in the Handbook is very marked: if both were used in the same class, the disparity of the responses would raise issues about equality of opportunity.

Right from the Start (Hutchin, 1999) contains a set of questions to ask parents which was devised as a result of talking to a wide range of practitioners. These questions provide a good half-way house between the parent conference prompts and the parent questionnaire in the Profile Handbook. In the LEA I currently work for, we recommend that all early years settings and schools use these and practitioners have found them very useful, either as a questionnaire or as a prompt to initial discussions with parents.

The best time to hold this discussion is on a home visit or parent's first visit to the school. If it is carried out in a school nursery class, it does not need to be exactly repeated in the reception class, but a discussion with parents about their child's interests and involvement at home is just as important in the new class and needs to be recorded in the same way. The expectation for the Profile is that parents should be involved in creating a 'shared picture' of their child from the beginning of their time in the setting 'in which assessments are completed', so reception teachers will need to plan these discussions.

Involving the parents: examples

The various schools from which the observations and children's work have been taken for the purposes of this book involve parents in their ongoing assessment processes. The methods they use are frequently revised to ensure a high level of involvement from all parents, and many settings regularly ask parents for feedback as part of the evaluation of their systems. The following example comes from one of the schools.

Andrea, from one of the schools discussed in the next chapter, told me:

> ❛ *We encourage parents to spend the first 15 minutes of the day with us, playing with their child, looking at their learning diaries. We have a parent conference once per term, where we explain how much we respect their knowledge of their own child. We realise that the child might be very different at home – for example much more confident at talking. Also the parents see our documentation on the wall. The children show it to their parents and so do we. Parents often ask for copies of the photos. Some parents write up their observations and comments about their children, others just tell us and we put it on a sticker, stating that the parent told us this.* ❜

Elise (in reception) and her mother wanted to share some typical home experiences.

Parent's Voice

A LEARNING STORY: I love Sunday mornings

Child's Name: Elise (Reception Class)

Date: 9th March

Elise likes to make cakes with her Nanny on Sunday mornings. In this picture Elise is making M and M cakes. She asked if she could wear a chef's hat so her Nan improvised with an apron.
Elise did almost everything herself. Emptying the mix into the bowl, adding the egg and the water. Then she mixed all the ingredients together with a wooden spoon. Her Nan finished off by whisking the ingredients together.
Elise likes to put the mixture into the cake cases. The real reason she likes to make cakes is that she loves to taste the mixture in the bowl whilst the cakes are baking in the oven. Yum! Yum!

The Child's Voice

Child's Name: Elise		A LEARNING STORY
Date: 11th March		
Belonging	TAKING AN INTEREST	I asked Elise to come over and look at the photograph.
Wellbeing	BEING INVOLVED	*'I am baking at my Nan's house. I have a bowl and a baking spoon because I am baking a cake and it's chocolate with sprinkles on the top – chocolate ones. I am wearing a dressing gown and an apron on my head.'*
Exploration	PERSISTING WITH DIFFICULTY	
Communication	EXPRESSING AN IDEA OR FEELING	*'Why are you wearing an apron on your head?'* I asked. *'Because it's like a baking head – no, hat. I mean a baking hat!'*
Contribution	TAKING RESPONSIBILITY	*'Can I go and play with the playdough now?'*

Writing comments in this way presents such a great opportunity to celebrate the kind of significant learning which takes place as a matter of course at home. The 'Child's Voice' was recorded at school by her teacher. The 'story' was mounted on a wall display with the photograph and many other comments from the parent and the teacher. The parent's comments gave some more background information to how Elise is at home, and how she felt she had developed in many positive ways since being at school. The teacher's comments were about the skills, understanding and dispositions she felt that Elise was demonstrating in this whole event.

Why involve the children?

Throughout this book the importance of talking to young children about their learning has been highlighted. In Chapter 4 informal conversations with children were flagged up as one kind of evidence to be added to the records of learning. The Foundation Stage Profile 'child interview' is rather different, as it is about a deliberate conversation helping the children to reflect back on their development. Both elements of involving children are equally important. In both *Tracking Significant Achievement in the Early Years* (Hutchin, 1996) and *Right from the Start* (Hutchin, 1999), involving children in many different ways was noted as a significant strand of assessment. In most of the case studies in Chapter 6, the staff were either already involving children through child conferences or interviews, or were about to begin to develop these. Such practice is essential if assessment is to make a positive difference to learning: it is about changing assessment from something which is *done to* the child to something which is *done with* the child.

Over the past two decades, involving young children in their own assessment, at least at times of transition from one class to another, has been happening in a growing number of schools and settings. The practice first became established in London, for example, in the mid-1980s with the *Primary Language Record*. This asked teachers to complete a 'child conference' at the beginning and again at the end of the year, about her/his own development in literacy. Although designed for primary classrooms, it was found to be just as applicable in the early years and continued to be promoted in early years settings by some LEAs, long after the *Primary Language Record* itself was superseded.

The benefits of involving the children

Some teachers have expressed concern about the amount of time such a practice might take, but in terms of teaching, the benefits to the children are enormous and it needs to be seen as a core part of teaching. As Pat Gura and Lorraine Hall (2000) wrote: *'adult-supported self-assessment is a way of working with children, not an add-on.'* What is more, it gives some important insights into the children's own thinking. Here are some examples.

In a nursery class, the teacher interviewed **Lily**, aged 4½ years. This is an extract from the interview.

Teacher: 'What do you like best about our nursery?'

Lily: 'When everybody gives me stories. I like playing with my friends (names them). We play babies and we have to catch Conor but we can't because he keeps running away!'

Teacher: '*What do you think you are learning when you come to nursery?*'

Lily: '*Counting. I have already learnt sharing. I learn my name.*'

Teacher: '*What do you think you are really good at?*'

Lily: '*I am good at painting, I'm good at cutting'.*'

Teacher: '*What do you find hard at school?*'

Lily: '*Sometimes it's hard to write my name. I just like playing with everything. You know, at home it's boring and I like coming to school.*'

Conor, in the same nursery, answered the question about what was hard in this way:

'*You know what I find really hard? Writing my name. I can't count to a 100, but I can count to 16.*'

Shelley-Anne: Reception class

The Child's Voice

Child's Name: Shelley-Anne **Date:** 3rd April	**A LEARNING STORY**

Belonging	TAKING AN INTEREST	Shelley-Anne was very keen to look at her own record. She pointed to a photo, '*It was me and Josie. Josie is in front of me and I'm at the back and we're dancing to the music thing.*'
Wellbeing	BEING INVOLVED	She looked at the next picture, '*I was reading "We're going on a Bear Hunt".*' She turned to a photo of a money sorting activity she had done. '*I got them in the right place. There's my group working with me!*'
Exploration	PERSISTING WITH DIFFICULTY	
Communication	EXPRESSING AN IDEA OR FEELING	'*It's me writing, this one. I was writing about the Bear Hunt.*' She began to recite the chorus of the story.
Contribution	TAKING RESPONSIBILITY	'*And there, that's me tidying up, isn't it?*' she said proudly. She laughed at the next picture, '*Why do I have that picture in my book, I'm wearing wellies!*'

What are the best ways of interviewing children?

Pat Gura and Lorraine Hall (2000) have written about talking to children of nursery age about their own learning during the normal course of learning opportunities and activities. They discuss how children are already involved in reflecting on themselves in all sorts of ways, such as poring over photographs of themselves and their friends. They recommend ways of talking with children which helps them to self-evaluate. For example: '. . . *asking a child "what do you like about your work?" seems more effective that "tell me about your work".'*

In the book *Listening to Four Year Olds*, Jacqui Cousins (1999) interviewed and listened in other less formal ways to over 100 four-year-olds. The book makes wonderful reading, giving the reader an insight into how children understand the world and an opportunity to consider the implications for practitioners. One of her interview techniques involved using a tape recorder in a pretend studio which children had an opportunity to play with, interviewing each other before she began. Others she observed and recorded in many different situations as well as asking them direct questions.

However, in most cases, particularly for most children towards the end of their time in reception, an interview can be a special opportunity to sit down with one child and offer her/him your full attention. For many, the best strategy is just being willing to listen and to take seriously what they say, by writing it down or recording it. It does need to be planned as a part of the planned teaching, or it is likely to be forgotten or pushed out by other demands. The examples here were collected in this way, without the use of a tape recorder or other aids.

Asking the questions

Looking through the child's portfolio, record or learning diary which includes their samples of work can be the best starting point, focusing the child on things they have done in the past. Photographs, as many of the practitioners in the case studies say, are the most powerful way of helping children to reflect on their learning. Gura and Hall point out that in ongoing self-assessment, designed to encourage children to become more reflective on their learning, questions need to be kept to a minimum and when questions are asked, '. . . *time should be allowed for children to think about how they will answer.*'

In an interview, however, open-ended questions will be needed. The *Foundation Stage Profile Handbook* gives some questions and prompts which could be used as a guide, but the following should elicit the kinds of reflective answers you are seeking:

What do you like doing best at home/at nursery/school?

What do you think you can do now that you couldn't do before/when you were younger?

What do you think you learn (or learn about) at nursery/school?

What do you learn (or learn about) at home?

What do you think you are really good at doing?

What do you find hard to do or don't like to do?

Have you any favourite toys/books/games/videos/songs, etc?

Carrying out the interviews

Interviews will need to be carried out sensitively and the situation you set up in which to do this may well affect the child. Knowing the children well will of course help, so that the situation can be made most comfortable for them. For some this may mean sitting comfortably in the book area, whilst for others it may mean being outside or in their favourite play area, or role play of the sort described by Jacqui Cousins. Another technique is to get the children themselves to photograph what is significant or enjoyable to them. This method is especially useful for children who may not be communicating verbally. A research project on listening to children's perspectives in their daily lives, written up in *Listening to Young Children: The Mosaic Approach*, by Clark and Moss (2001), describes how using many different techniques and fitting them together like a mosaic can be the best approach to gain a more in-depth and less of a snapshot view.

Jessica, a child in a reception class, was generally shy in speaking to adults in school, but she was happy to look through her record with a visitor, as we sat outside on the grass. It was clear that what was significant to her as we looked through her diary was her development in writing skills. She laughed aloud when she saw how she had written the *'a'* in her name a year before. She read out her 'Bear Hunt' story and showed how pleased she was with her developing achievements in literacy. When asked how she learnt to write like this, she said: *'I just try and try it.'* It was quite clear from her actions afterwards that skipping and hopping (doing both at the same time!) was an important new achievement which she was busy practising: *'I can hop and do it. Look, I CAN do it!'*

Interviewing younger children may produce less evaluative talk, as very few will have much experience of being asked to be reflective in this way. They are likely to talk about things that are immediate – for example, something they see around them or have just been involved in. Even so, they may reveal what is important to them, at that moment in time, and often this reflects something of a deeper importance in their development. Once children become familiar with this practice and have a better understanding of the vocabulary in the questions, they become more able to reflect on their own learning.

With some younger and less verbal children, as well as children who are new to English, careful framing of the questions may be required, but the important thing is to *try* – if there is no response, try changing how you ask the question. For example, in one nursery school the teacher asked a series of questions including the question *'What do you learn at nursery?'* She discovered that, of the children she interviewed, not many understood the key word. Four-year-old Taisa, for example, at an early stage in speaking in English, did not appear to understand the word *learn*, but the moment the question was changed to *'What do you think people teach you at nursery?'*, she said: *'For play with blocks, for play with pen.'* With a similar question about what she is taught at home, she said: *'For do letters – number 4, number 6, number 7, number 11.'*

Julia, a shy child who did not until recently initiate conversations with adults at nursery and who was also quiet with other children, felt more at ease being 'interviewed' once her record of achievement was produced for her to see. She mentioned things to do with her learning at home which the staff were not aware of: *'I do some homework – I do pluses. My Dad writes them on the paper and I do it with peas.'*

Such comments are really useful for staff. Knowing what she sees as significant learning at home can have a two-fold benefit. First, staff at nursery can build on her skills. Second, getting her to be the expert and share her skills is likely to raise her self-esteem and confidence.

Abedalamir, who we met in Chapter 4, was asked the questions below. His first language is Arabic, but after four terms in nursery his English is increasingly fluent.

What do you like doing best at nursery?

'I like playing with J. in the garden . . . kick football.'

He also added: 'I like jumping and writing.'

Do you learn things at nursery? 'Writing.'

What do you find hard? 'Writing.'

What do you learn at home? 'Arabic writing with my mum.'

It is interesting how significant writing seems to be in nursery- and reception-age children, although this is not unpredictable considering how much emphasis there is on it in school and in many homes! Here Abedalamir not only states how he likes to do it, but that it is hard. Lily and Conor too, from another nursery, said it was hard. Another nursery child, Jaime, also mentioned writing as something he learnt at nursery. In this small sample of children, all but one of the children mentioned writing or numbers, or both, in answer to the questions about learning and teaching, yet none of the writing or number 'work' in these nurseries is taught in a formal way: every learning experience is play-based.

The two strands to this chapter have been about ensuring that the most important people to be involved in contributing to the Profile – the child and her/his parents or principal carers – have a central role to play. The examples show some of the ways that practitioners are already doing this: they are also fulfilling the expectations of the Foundation Stage Profile.

With regard to parents there is a requirement in every school year for parents to receive a report on their child's progress and a time to meet with teachers to discuss the report. Involving them in contributing their views on their child's development will make this a much more inclusive process. The benefits to children's learning

Fig 5.1 *Abedalamir writing about Bob the Builder*

and your understanding of them are huge: children begin to see themselves as learners and have the opportunity to reflect on their own strategies and problem solving skills. There is also another advantage to self-assessment – not only do we get an insight into their thinking, it also demonstrates that we value their opinions.

Let us leave the last word to a parent and child. The parent wrote:

❝ *This report has captured Callum beautifully. He has had an exciting fun- and play-filled year at nursery. He has grown emotionally and socially whilst maintaining his enthusiasm and active zest for life.* ❞

Callum himself said:

❝ *I like playing on the bikes. I am good at running and jumping and bouncing a ball.* ❞

Record-keeping systems in action: some case studies

6

One of the most useful strategies when coming to grips with a new way of working is to visit other settings to see different practice in action, sharing new ideas. It can either confirm that what you are doing is on the right lines or help to give you new ways forward. This is exactly the purpose of this chapter – to share some record-keeping and assessment systems that some foundation stage practitioners and their schools have developed.

These 'case studies' show a breadth of different types of foundation stage provision. They are not a representative sample of practice in England, but individual settings where practitioners have developed their assessment systems according to their different circumstances and staffing arrangements. However, what they have in common is a belief in the foundation stage and the importance of observing. They also show that there are some exciting changes taking place in England in early years assessment – many of these motivated by an interest in developments in early years practice in an international context rather than instigated by the Foundation Stage Profile.

All of the settings keep their approaches under review, developing them in the light of their evaluations. Although the nursery school is less affected by the Foundation Stage Profile, they all share the view that the Profile is in many respects in line with their ongoing processes of assessment. Three of the case studies (the nursery school and two of the primary schools) have been greatly influenced by the pre-schools of Reggio Emilia in Italy and the New Zealand early years curriculum, *Te Whariki*, described in Chapter 2. They have also been influenced by new developments in New Zealand in assessment practice: the idea of Learning Stories.

The Learning Stories approach

In 2001, Margaret Carr published a book describing a new approach to early years assessment in New Zealand. The New Zealand early years curriculum focuses attention on developing children's positive dispositions to learning, motivation and social development, but in general, assessment practice was not in line with this approach. Margaret Carr, one of the directors of the curriculum working group, began to develop new assessment processes with a group of practitioners.

She was interested in the idea of developing narrative observations, which she called *Learning Stories*, to document children's learning:

> *The stories included the context, they often include the relationship with adults and peers, they highlighted the activity or task at hand . . . and . . . an interpretation from a storyteller who knew the child well and focused on evidence of new or sustained interest, involvement, challenge, communication or responsibility.*

The assessment process used in the Learning Stories she calls the '4 Ds of assessment': *describing* (what has been observed), *discussing* (with colleagues and others), *documenting* (writing it up) and *deciding* (what to do next). The stories concentrate on what is significant, but they tell a story and so are longer than the short, quick note-type of observation.

One aspect of this approach which has most interested the practitioners in these case studies is the idea of documenting the learning process to a wider audience than just their own staff, by displaying their Learning Stories for all to see, as well as adding to the children's records. They have adopted and adapted elements from the Reggio Emilia and New Zealand approaches, alongside what they were already doing in addressing the foundation stage. All three settings described here have done this independently of each other, tailored to their own situations. The other case studies have developed their assessment practices too, and all of them show how convinced they are about the power of observing play as a tool to planning, making the curriculum fit the child rather than the other way round. In all of the case studies, the development of the digital camera has made a big difference, making photography much less expensive and more accessible. As Dilwen put it: *'photographs speak volumes when it comes to observing.'*

CASE STUDIES

A primary school with a nursery class and an early years centre attached

This school, situated in an area of high unemployment on the outskirts of a major city, has a social services family centre for 'children in need' incorporated into it, along with other supportive services for families with young children, creating an Early Years Centre. The record-keeping systems described here with regard to the nursery and reception classes also apply to the Early Years Centre. The team leader and nursery class teacher, Andrea, has been strongly influenced by a visit to Reggio Emilia and by Margaret Carr's Learning Stories.

The focal point of the record-keeping is each child's Learning Diary. Evidence of learning is kept in individual Learning Diaries for each child – A4 booklets with a photograph of the child on the front. They contain the observations as well as samples and photographs. They are kept in zip wallets hanging on the children's coat pegs for easy access by the family as well as the child. The children frequently talk about them. Sometimes they are put out on the table in the classroom, to ensure that parents and children do look at them together.

All staff carry out observations on any child, but take responsibility for a small group each. Andrea told me: *'The observation process is well established now, and we are trying to improve by making sure that the observations and assessments are not just describing what the child is doing in a lot of detail, but focus on the actual learning. Our "Learning Map" has helped a lot with this.'*

The aim of producing the Learning Map was to support staff with a range of levels of qualifications and skills to share a common view of what development and progress in learning looks like.

'I created the Learning Map using a range of documents to form a picture of what children's learning is really like. I used Planning for Progress *(Tower Hamlets Early Years Curriculum Guidelines), the* Curriculum Guidance for the Foundation Stage, Te Whariki *because of its emphasis on dispositions, as well as the National Literacy and National Numeracy Strategy folders, because reception teachers have to pay attention to these elements of teaching too. The map includes the Stepping Stones and Early Learning Goals but creates a much fuller picture. It shows the real breadth*

of learning – the knowledge, skills, understanding and attitudes we hope children will learn – and we also use it for the learning objectives in our planning.'

But Andrea felt that some really important learning was going unrecorded. The Learning Diaries were very much about individuals and the documentation about particular projects. An essential element of learning – the 'socially constructed' or group learning, where children collaborate and learn together – was not in evidence or being celebrated. This is where the Learning Stories come in.

'Some learning events turn into a significant ongoing project. If staff feel that there is more going on than could be put on stickers, because it is a group doing things together and the learning event or play is more involved, then it will become a Learning Story. We also document it in detail through wall displays, photos of the learning in process, and things the children have made associated with it. The majority of things which we document in this way arise out of interests of the children.'

Unlike the stickers, which are written on immediately and then placed in the diaries, the Learning Stories are written up afterwards at the end of the day. The reception teachers find this documentation very valuable: *'It has had great benefits for building up relationships with parents, especially for those parents who aren't able to get so involved. They are so pleased when they see what is really going on at school.'*

The story does not end here. They have also introduced some of Margaret Carr's other ideas, such as the 'Child's Voice' and the 'Parents Voice': examples of both can be seen in Chapter 5.

One final but important strand to the assessment and planning cycle here is the daily, planned adult-led activities. In the nursery, for example, each member of staff plans a focused activity for the children in their key group, specifically addressing their interests, learning styles and needs. Detailed observations are written on the planning sheet for these 'adult-framed' activities, noting how the individual children approached the activity, particular aspects which interested the child as well as anything significant the child said. This is also taken into account when the records are reviewed and summarised.

Group Stories

Children: Aaron, Amy, Zoe, Jasmine, Richard & Tyler
Date: 27.9.02
Observer: AS & SG

Involvement indicators	Decision points and examples of cues in the learning story	THE LEARNING STORY
belonging	**TAKING AN INTEREST:** finding an interest *here* - a topic, an activity, a role. Recognising the familiar, <u>enjoying the unfamiliar</u>. Coping with <u>change.</u>	We introduced the OHP to the children to enhance their play experiences in the 'Lets Pretend' area. We planned to support the children's first experience with the OHP, so that they would feel confident to use it independently in the future.
well-being	**BEING INVOLVED:** paying attention for a <u>sustained period, feeling safe, trusting others.</u> Being playful with <u>others and/or materials</u>	The group of children chose to come and explore the new apparatus. Aaron said 'Oh look, wow!' and Zoe said 'Look' in response to the light reflecting on the wall. Tyler watched the other
exploration	**PERSISTING WITH DIFFICULTY:** setting and choosing difficult tasks. Using a range of strategies to solve problems when 'stuck' (be specific)	children placing objects on the top of the OHP. Zoe asked Tyler "What's happening?". Zoe then asked "What's videoing?" as more jewels were placed on the top of the projector. Richard & Aaron were very excited and began
communication	**EXPRESSING AN IDEA OR A FEELING:** in a range of ways (specify). For example: <u>oral language,</u> gesture, music, art, writing, using numbers and patterns, telling stories.	jumping up and down. Aaron seemed to make the connection between the objects & the shadows on the wall. He commented 'Isn't that a mess' pointing to the wall. Aaron then took some objects to the wall & held them up to the wall. Aaron told us he 'was trying to light them up but it didn't'. Tyler began to explore the objects as some children moved
contribution	**TAKING RESPONSIBILTY:** responding to others, to stories, and imagined events, ensuring that things are fair, self-evaluating, helping others, contributing to the curriculum	away. 'Ah diamonds' he said & Amy copied his language repeating 'diamonds'. Amy and Tyler continued to rearrange the objects on the OHP, then selected new objects to use.

Short Term Review	What Next?
• curiosity & excitement to learn • cooperation & using language to express ideas/connect thinking • operating simple ICT apparatus • confidence to try new activities • selecting range of resources **Question:** what learning did I think went on here (i.e. the main point(s) of the learning story)?	• use transparancies with OHT • encourage children to make shadow puppets • regularly change resources in the projector area. Questions: How might we encourage this interest, ability, strategy, disposition, learning story to be: ♦ More complex ♦ Appear in different areas or activities of the curriculum/classroom How might we encourage the next 'step' in the learning story framework?

Fig 6.1 A group Learning Story

Projected Learning Intention(s):		Activity/Experience:		Date & Adult:	
Explore shape & form in 3D → 2D → 3D Develop confidence to sketch & design (Cr) Identify and name ☐ and count accurately → 4 (Ma)		Look at selection of 3 small chairs & a stool from front, side & back. Ask children to design their own 2D chairs for making into 3D with clay		28.1.03 Andrea	
Brandon / ~~Hannah~~	~~Jordan~~ / Aaron /	Lilli / Jess	Katherine / Hannah	Richard	Reflections & Assessments
Brandon: 'I can't do it' 'I've done the seat' (used a palmar grip)	drew ☐, then ☐ and [123] 'I'm doing numbers on mine' 'I'm doing a granks chair' coloured over designs 'It's a little tiny ants chair' Jordan: drew circle like shapes filled the space of his page confidently	Lilli: 'I'm doing the back 1st', I've got a baby chair and a big one 2nd back Jess: drew some circles, then swathes of broad strokes	Katherine: 'I'm doing the legs' Watched the other children before committing to paper Hannah: 'I've done a chair, show everyone Andrea!'	4 sits so you don't fall off. 'I've done a bigger one' Confident lines & approach.	• Richard has a strong sense of detail & design He was able to talk about his work and give an explanation for an element of his design. • Aaron was able to write numeral 1–4 – he used detail in his design – needed adult support when he was dissatisfied. Aaron happy to take prompt from another child – socially constructed learning • Lilli worked very independently & confidently. Added more detail with 2nd chair. • Brandon initially reluctant but with adult encouragement he had a go. • Hannah was delighted after seeming to be dissatisfied. • Jess & Jordan worked quietly – lots of circle shapes • Katherine not confident but accurate with legs. TA: Smaller group for design in clay (2 × 5)

Fig 6.2 *Andrea's adult framed planning sheet*

A nursery school in an urban area

Over the last few years in this school, an important focus for development has been sharing children's records with parents and the children themselves. Every child has a 'Special Folder' which documents the significant developments she/he is making at nursery and at home, through photographs, samples, captions and the child's own comments. The folders are kept on low, open shelves accessible to the children and parents. Each folder has the child's photograph and name on the cover and as a starting point, linking nursery with home, children are encouraged to bring in a favourite photo or two from home.

Each member of staff is key worker to a group of children, responsible for developing the folders of the children in her/his

Fig 6.3 *Louise looking at her special folder*

group, ensuring that other records are up to date. They use the LEA's foundation stage Record of Achievement, writing observations onto sticky labels and adding them to the children's records under the appropriate areas of learning.

> **Vishal**, aged 4, commented on his folder as he showed it to me:
>
> V: *'That's me – when I was a little baby – look'*. He particularly liked showing me his painting. *'Someone helped me to cut it out. When my teacher came to my house I made this.'* When I asked him what was his favourite thing in the folder he told me: *'I like this one'*, pointing to a family photograph.

A visit to Reggio Emilia by the deputy head, Sue, resulted in some new developments: *'We saw the way they developed projects with the children based on their interests and documented this learning. We felt that this type of documentation was such a good way to share children's learning with parents, visitors and the children themselves.'*

Joseph enjoyed careful experimentation with the powder paints. He deliberately mixed colours together to make many different shades. *'I'm going to mix blue with red. Yellow and red, that's made dark orange. It's gone green. That's magic isn't it? I'm making red, but when I put in blue it's made a purply kind of blue.'*

Fig 6.4 *A learning story about Joseph's colour mixing*

Further developments took place after hearing about Margaret Carr's Learning Stories and the nursery began to use these to document significant moments as they happened. The stories are written up on the computer from the observational notes taken at the time, alongside the digital photographs. Already a parent who regularly helps in the nursery has become involved in writing Learning Stories too. Penny, the headteacher, summed up the documentation process thus: *'The whole thing is about sharing our enthusiasm for learning in an informed way.'*

A primary school in the suburbs on the edge of a rural area

This school, with its double unit nursery and three reception classes working closely together, has similar observation, assessment and record-keeping methods to the nursery school, but across the whole foundation stage. A visit to Reggio Emilia by the headteacher had also been influential.

A Learning Story

Natalie built a tower with wooden bricks and fitted play people inside, playing out a story with the figures going in and out of doors. The next day she spent 30 minutes carefully drawing a picture of a house and took it to the block area. *'I've finished my drawing. I want to build the house using bricks. It doesn't matter that they're not coloured'. 'I need to build it where it won't get knocked down.'* She propped up her plan and started to build, adding people and telling the story as she went. *'There are loads of people in the garage. One in the bath, one sitting on the toilet. Now there's two in the bath – it's a big bath.'*

Natalie balanced the bricks carefully to make rooms. At one point there were three in the bed, but they kept rolling off, so she patiently tried using different bricks to resolve the problem. The story continued and the house developed in more and more complex ways. Other children came to watch, and she said to them. *'I'm making a house, you can copy it'*, referring to her plan. Hannah came over to see what Natalie was doing. She decided they would need to order more bricks. *'I've got the number, so I've ordered some more bricks'*, she said as she made a telephone call. *'4 bricks, please'*, then she looked at the house, *'A whole packet of bricks.'* And Natalie added: *'Hello, a hundred bricks.'*

The nursery teacher and early years coordinator, Anna, felt that the children's portfolios, containing the samples and photographs, were a significant part of their record-keeping. Recently the foundation stage classes introduced Learning Stories too. The staff here felt that the most important aspect of the planning and assessment system is the daily, detailed discussions between staff about the children. This affects what they plan and provide for the following days and weeks.

Fig 6.5 Natalie's block play

An inner city primary school with a nursery class

The foundation stage classes in this school consist of two reception classes and a nursery class. The early years coordinator, Dilwen, began to introduce the use of observations and creating individual 'profiles' for the children when she started working in the school four years before. The profiles in this school are the children's individual records, containing all the observations, samples and photographs, regular reviews and conferences with parents: *'I introduced the new system with regular training at weekly meetings and training days. I also began to do paired observations with every member of staff – both of us observing the same child for five minutes or so and then discussing our observations.'*

Setting up the system with a large and changing team, new to this way of working, required frequent discussions as well as ongoing training. For example, staff needed to be clear about the difference between the observation and the assessment, so that they wrote down what had happened and not just their judgements: *'Another issue was ensuring that assessments were written positively, so that staff were writing what children can do rather than can't. We talked at length about the terminology we use and the importance of useful phrases such as "can do with support".'*

Their assessment system consists of incidental observations on stickers, participant observations and planned, focused observations, where a member of staff stands back and observes children in their own free choice of activity. Each focused observation takes about ten minutes. Dilwen's aim was to do one of these on every child every half-term, but it usually turns out to happen once a term. When asked which part of the assessment system proved to be most useful for informing planning, the focused observations won the day:

'We have a set time to do these, on one afternoon a week. We aim to observe 5 children during the afternoon, but with interruptions, it is more usual to do 3. We analyse them at the end of the day after school, and the assessments go straight into the profiles, in the appropriate areas of learning. They are fascinating because they tell us so much, especially about who the child interacts with, how they play in group situations and persevere with things. Doing them regularly means you see how they change during the year.

'Sharing records with the parents is the best thing. We review each child's record every half-term and set learning priorities from these for the child. We meet with parents once a term and the review sheets would go home to parents, so that they could see how their child had progressed, with a letter saying they are welcome to come and ask us more about it. We always show the whole profile to the parents and encourage them to take the profiles home for the weekend to show the rest of the family. Parents really appreciate them.'

Child's name *Oscar*

Fircroft Early Years
December Half Term Review

Progress since last half term

* Plays with a range of peers as well as 'special' friend.
* Is able to subtract using numbers 6-10. Can partition mentally to takeaway.
- Knows at least 13 sounds, 25 letter names and 5 high frequency words
* Has made models in workshop using encyclopedia and own ideas before making eg flag & flag pole.

Targets for next half term

* To climb over an A frame.
* To write a sentence and use a full stop.
* To add and subtract to 20 (and decide which operation to use)

Teacher's signature D. Ndzevb

Date 3/01/02

Fig 6.6

An independent school which will be using the Profile

In an independent school with one reception class and no nursery, the reception teacher, Sarah, has recently developed her record-keeping and assessment system with a new observation format, making use of digital photographs. The photograph becomes the centrepiece of the observation and a starting point for a detailed analysis of the child's learning observed: *'I used to use the "record of achievement" produced by our local LEA, which was a format for collecting observations with a "what next" column. I never used that column. . . . This kind of observation is giving me a much better understanding of the child. By evaluating the learning in the photograph, it reinforces for me what the children can do.'*

Her detailed analysis of these observations has made the implications for planning flow more easily than before: *'It makes me think of a way forward, often making links with what the child may be doing at home.'*

Her aim is to do one of these longer observations each half-term per child. Rather than start out with a list of names which she goes through automatically, after a few weeks into the term she makes a list of children she has observed. In this way she has picked up learning events which seem to be significant, and the list shows who she needs to focus on, looking more closely for significant events:

'The assessments don't take long now, about 10 minutes for each one, usually at the end of the day. When I take the photograph I also make notes on what was happening, as a prompt. I then put the photo onto the computer in the classroom and begin the analysis, with the photo in the centre of the page, usually at the end of the day. The great thing is that I can show it to the child – they will sometimes come to the computer with me to look at the photos and talk about what was happening.'

Her system is still developing – for example, at the time of my discussion with her, Sarah felt that she needed to include more about the background to the event observed, as this would set it in context.

There are other aspects to Sarah's assessment system. Each child has a Special Achievement Book, in which the stickers (notes on the 'landmarks' she notices) and the photo observations are kept, along with a child interview. She also keeps notes from her adult-led activities and samples of work, writing assessment comments on the work, so that she can share these with the children. Each aspect of her record-keeping system fulfils a different purpose. When asked what was most useful to her teaching, Sarah responded: *'The photo observations are proving to be the most powerful in terms of understanding the child better. They have personalised the record-keeping to the child'.*

A special school

The school caters for children with severe learning difficulties from age 2 to age 19. In a special school such as this, the assessment process involves a large number of people, such as therapists and school subject leaders, as well as the class staff. Assessment information is recorded in many different ways. The most important document for each child is the Individual Education Plan (IEP). The early years manager, Lesley, and the headteacher, Tina, described their assessment processes:

'Each child has an IEP designed to meet her or his specific needs, incorporating targets for each area of learning. Every child will be given one or more structured sessions per day to work specifically on some of their IEP targets, and observations of achievements towards these targets will be made on special IEP recording sheets stored in the child's folder.'

The foundation stage class has also devised a complementary system for assessment where other significant developments are recorded, as staff work with the children throughout the day.

'Each child has a clipboard with six recording sheets, one for each area of learning. This is where we record significant achievements. Children receive certificates for significant achievements and these go home, so that the child can celebrate the success with the parents.

'We also do short two-minute observations of children during play periods inside and outside, concentrating on recording what we see occurring, and not at this stage interpreting it in any way. We mainly look out for children's communication, interaction and investigation strategies in these.'

There are also assessments of the child's progress in communication and language, appropriate to the particular system the child is using – for example, the Picture Exchange Communication System (PECS). Every child's record is monitored once per fortnight to

Hettie – 11/03/03   Age: 5.1

Personal, Social and Emotional Development
- Hettie is able to play for sustained periods at games of her creation
- Hettie enjoys playing with her peers. Here she is playing a gardening game with Louisa.

Communication, Language and Literacy
- Hettie is able to communicate effectively with her peers.
- Hettie is able to explain what she is doing to the teacher: "We're making bean plants."

Mathematical Development
- Hettie is able to use appropriate positional language to describe her actions: "Two on the top. One on the bottom."

Knowledge and Understanding of the World
- Hettie know that plants need water in order to grow: "They grow a lot because we water them every day.
- Hettie knows that seeds grow into plants: "They grow into bean plants."

Physical Development
- Hettie is able to pour water carefully from a watering can

Creative Development
- Hettie is able to play in role for sustained periods. "I'm watering my bean plants."

Implications for Planning
- Hettie will be invited to bring in books about planting, seed packets and other gardening items.
- Hettie will continue to observe her beans growing in the classroom.

Fig 6.7 Sarah's photo observation and assessment format (observation of Hettie)

CURRICULUM RECORDING

Pupil's name: ....Paul...

Subject: .......P.S.E. Development...................................

Date	Topic	P Level	Comments/Achievements/Progress	Teacher initial
13/2/03	Cookery		Paul loved tasting the saltanas. He tried very hard to use the whisk + managed several half rotations. Found it difficult to remain seated.	L R
6/3/03	Cookery.		Paul loved the porridge. He enjoyed tasting it dry, and when milk was added. Paul was good at stirring the milk in, and used his spoon to eat the porridge.	PB.

Fig 6.8 *Curriculum recording sheet*

identify any gaps and plan to address these. All the records are reviewed at the end of every term.

New and exciting developments are also happening with the introduction of the Foundation Stage Profile. In meetings with parents to discuss children's progress, such as the annual IEP reviews, the staff have always put up displays of photographs and observation notes showing the child's progress.

'We are now beginning to create individual portfolios, to help children celebrate their achievements and evaluate their work. The portfolios contain art work, observations, annotated digital photographs and copies of the significant achievement certificates. Children will be able to contribute to these by choosing their preferred samples, for example, by selecting from two shown to them. The staff will talk to them about the portfolios and encourage the children to respond through eye-contact, facial expressions, vocalisations, speech, signs or gestures as appropriate.'

In terms of summative assessment, the school has found the 'P Scales' most effective. These are the QCA assessment scales which describe in general terms levels of achievements of children working towards Level 1 of the National Curriculum. Although the statements are geared to the National Curriculum rather than the Foundation Stage, it has still been useful in the early years. The school has worked on extending these, to create further steps within each level. But the Foundation Stage Profile is still considered very important. *'We must ensure our children are included in the foundation stage.'*

Developing record-keeping processes

These case studies show examples of some of the developments which were already taking place in early years settings with regard to assessment. I am grateful to the practitioners in these case studies for sharing their experiences and systems of assessment processes. Carrying out observations is seen by all staff in these schools as part of their normal daily work. These staff teams share a desire to continually evaluate and improve their assessment and record-keeping, to ensure that children's achievements are celebrated and learning processes are documented in greater depth. They also share a determination to find the best ways to involve children and parents in the process, especially enabling children to reflect on their own learning. This is particularly challenging for the special school, whose team is working together to find appropriate ways to involve the children in the process.

The Foundation Stage Profile is also bringing with it new developments too. In another school with a well developed record-keeping system, from which some of the examples of observations and notes on achievements in Chapter 4 have been drawn, the early years coordinator, Lisa, said:

'Next term we are introducing a system of planned observations as we feel these will show us other things we are not recording. We intend to do one child per day in this way and this will ensure that we have at least one per child per term. We also want to start sharing the "work sample" files with the children, especially for the child interview in the Profile.'

Angela, the nursery nurse in reception, told me:

'We don't go anywhere without our clipboards and stickers. We have it with us all the time, so that you can get what you see written down at the time, there and then. You need to be fast at writing, and as for finding significant things, outside is best for that.'

Keeping track of progress 7

In Chapter 4, I recommended that every observation and sample is analysed not only to make an assessment of the child's learning, but also to include some implications for planning. If the ongoing assessment process is assessment *for* learning, these planning points need to feed into the daily and weekly curriculum planning. Planning is of course written in advance but it must be flexible to truly support learning. Making the link between assessment and planning cannot be left to chance – it needs a clearly defined system, a unified approach across the school's foundation stage. We saw in Chapter 6 that the case study schools had all devised their own ways of ensuring that the assessments they made really did feed into planning.

Linking assessment to planning

Planning in nursery and primary education is usually thought of as taking place in three timescales: *long term* – an overview of what it is intended that children will learn over their time in, for example, the foundation stage; *medium term* – what is to be planned for the next few weeks; and *short term* – the weekly and daily detailed plans. The process of linking assessment to planning is best viewed as taking place in two different ways and time scales. The first is on the immediate day-to-day level, responding to what has just happened today. The second is via regular reviews.

Day-to-day planning

Several of the teachers interviewed in the case studies talked about the importance of their staff team's daily discussions about the children, evaluating what had gone on during the session and adapting the plans accordingly for the following day – or even the rest of the week. Some class teams sit down together for ten minutes at the end of the day. Most nursery schools and many nursery classes meet every day in this way. Others talk as they are tidying up, and the teacher enters the points made on the planning sheet later. This kind of daily planning is important in both a nursery and reception setting, although it might look different, depending on the nature and size of the staff team.

What and how to evaluate

This kind of daily evaluation means discussing *briefly:*
- which independent and freely chosen activities and learning experiences seemed to hold the children's attention most and extended their learning, and which did not go so well;
- some of the observations made during the session;
- whether the learning intentions for adult-led activities were met, or what happened instead.

After this quick evaluation the planning for the following day is adjusted, making any changes to the provision for the more independent activities as well as the focused, adult-led activities. Usually it is the provision and type of activity that will be changed, not the learning intentions, as the purpose of the evaluation is to tune what is provided to the children.

In Dilwen's school, the two reception teachers work in this way. Their daily evaluation is an essential part of their planning. The medium-term planning, including the relevant literacy and maths objectives, is used to feed into the weekly overview. But the detailed plans for focused work, independent activities and areas of provision inside and outside are planned daily, based on their evaluations.

Figure 7.1 is a small excerpt of the indoor daily planning sheet, which included eight areas of provision, with another eight on the outdoor planning sheet. In the week shown here, the focus was around the story *Handa's Surprise* and the class tadpoles. Broad learning intentions are also included on the sheet (not shown here).

It is the discussion that is most important. There is no need to write everything down, but in the usual busy day much of the discussion may be forgotten, unless some things are recorded. Even if the teacher works alone, having a few minutes to plan for the next day, based on what has taken place today, is vital.

In reception classes with classroom assistants, it is not always possible for them to stay at the end of the session, and often their day finishes before the children's. In this case, another way has to be found for the transfer of information. For example, giving the

Day	Imaginary	Creative	Water	Construction	Workshop
Mon	Shop: making receipts and shopping lists *Lots of receipts being made: A, M and D*	Close observation of fruit *Lots of discussion, not*	Tapioca *Lots of interest esp. F and S – associated it with frogspawn*	Handa's Surprise Journey on mat *G, L and R made routes and found animals*	Tissue paper fruits: *no children here*
Tues	Continue: add more real fruit	Continue close obs – encourage painting	Put books on frog life cycle nearby and magnifiers	Add book to area and animals	Adult to demonstrate technique

(Evaluations are shown in italics.)   **Fig 7.1**

classroom assistant time to jot down a few notes in a notebook or in the 'evaluation box' on the planning sheet before she/he leaves. In addition, the observations made during the session by the classroom assistant could be coded in some way, such as marking with a highlighter those observations which need to affect what is planned for the next day. In the longer term, however, the role of the classroom assistant will need to be considered, so that she/he can be involved in discussions and planning meetings.

Reviewing children's records

The second level of linking assessment to planning is to review every child's record regularly, in order to look through what has been collected, note any gaps (for example an area or aspect of learning) and to make a more general assessment of the child's progress and development. It also ensures that the planning points from each observation, not already addressed in the daily evaluations, are brought together, ready to feed into what is planned. This is early years 'target setting', for every individual child. Often these are called *learning priorities*, to avoid the narrower focus inherent in the idea of a target which has to be met. The London Borough of Merton produced the format shown in Figure 7.2.

Reviewing the children's records does take time, and needs to be planned. Some practitioners try to do all their reviews once per half-term, others once per term. In a nursery setting where there are

Child's name:	Date:
What next? *(learning priorities)* * * *	
Planning: *play opportunities, learning experiences and strategies for staff*	

Fig 7.2

several team members taking responsibilities for reviewing a group of children, the staffing is usually sufficient for records to be reviewed once per half-term. But, whatever the setting, as a minimum, every child's record should be reviewed once per term.

In the case studies, Sarah, Andrea and Lesley mentioned that their intention was to interview the children before every review and complete a self-assessment form or 'Child's voice' at this time.

In Dilwen's school the reviews were sent to parents with a letter, encouraging them to take their child's record home for the weekend. Both strategies are invaluable and make the planning for child and parent involvement into a regular routine.

Setting the learning priorities or targets

The learning priorities need to be individual, geared to the child's specific needs. They must be achievable and relevant to the child's interests and learning styles, which may mean helping to expand these in new directions.

I recommend reviewing the records on a rolling programme, choosing up to five children per week, ensuring the necessary information from these is fed into the following week's plans (see *Right from the Start* for more details). This could be one per day, although practitioners may prefer to review all five together on one day after school to fit in with other meetings. Obviously, with new children, this can only be started after their first two months or so in the setting.

Reviewing a small number of records each week, rather than all the children in the same week, makes the link to planning more immediate and manageable. The targets are for the children, but it is the staff who ensure the planning makes them achievable. Much of the review can be timetabled into the normal day so that at the time of the child's self-assessment interview the child and practitioner or key worker are going through the record together, celebrating achievements and deciding what next. Children, especially in reception, can be very good at devising their own meaningful targets, once they are given the opportunity to be regularly involved in a self-assessment process.

In this nursery school, where several of the examples in Chapter 4 come from, the key workers write reviews on children's progress in every area of learning twice per year. This is done on a rolling programme. We have met Abedalamir before: Figure 7.3 shows some of his targets (as well as what the nursery will do to support him) from the reviews.

Date	Targets
November (two months after starting at nursery)	• To part happily from Mum and Dad • For nursery to provide opportunities for him to develop English and support his home language through Arabic tapes and alphabet) • To identify and name colours and shapes in English • To access all areas of the curriculum
March	• Share core story books at nursery in English and borrow books from school library. Mum to continue using Arabic for speaking and writing at home • Count in sequence to 10+ • Extend his use of computer: e.g. using keyboard
November	• Retell familiar stories using remembered words and phrases; make connections between spoken word and print • Write most letters in his name • Count with 1:1 correspondence to 10
March	• Continue to retell stories with books/props and acting them out, building on existing repertoire • Help him to develop awareness of rhyming words and linking sounds and letters both when he writes and when we scribe for him, building on his enthusiasm for writing • Encourage Arabic writing and use of Arabic in the nursery

Fig 7.3

In Dilwen's reception class, the reviews are carried out every half-term. There is always a literacy and numeracy target, and the third target is usually chosen in discussion with the child. Her format for reviews has two parts: *'Progress since last half-term'* followed by *'Targets for next half-term'*. Figures 7.4 and 7.5 are two examples of

Date	Targets
Anna *October*	• *To write my name using upper and lower case letters (Anna).* • *To subtract using numbers up to 10.* • *To have a go at guessing how many.* *(When estimating or hypothesising, Anna is reluctant to guess, fearing that she might be wrong, so needs to become more confident.)*
December	• *To solve mathematical problems with numbers 0–20, and know whether to add or subtract.* • *To write in sentences and use a full stop.* • *To climb a rope (Anna's target).*

Fig 7.4

Anna   FEBRUARY HALF-TERM REVIEW
Progress since last half-term

- Is able to write sentences using full stops.
- Is confident to make a guess or estimate.
- In practical situations is able to add/subtract when appropriate.
- Is able to climb a rope.
- Continues to contribute enthusiastically to all areas of the curriculum in whole class, group and individual situations.
- Reads orange level books fluently and will use a variety of decoding strategies on blue level books.

Targets for next half-term

- *To write sentences using upper case at the beginning.*
- *To add on numbers 0–9 mentally or using my fingers.*
- *To make a cake all by myself (Anna's target).*

Fig 7.5

the targets for one child, followed by one full review. The observations and samples in Anna's record clearly show the evidence of progress. As can be seen, the review is a good way of celebrating achievements.

In the special school, termly reviews as well as the ongoing monitoring of records are extremely important, ensuring small steps are noted and celebrated and the targets for development are adapted as necessary. There is the statutory annual review and the termly review – which include a detailed summary for each area of learning – the communication and language assessment review, and others, according to the needs of the child. All of these are monitored once per fortnight.

One of Devano's termly targets is: *'To increase the control and co-ordination of small hand movements.'* One aspect of planning for him specifically relates to this: *'To increase use of arms to make small movements to move balloons or lentils in a tray. . . .'* Figure 7.6 shows Devano able to achieve this target.

Fig 7.6 *Devano achieves his target*

Making summative judgements in nursery and reception

The daily evaluations and termly or half-termly reviews of the whole record ensure an effective system of assessment *for* learning, using the same processes for both nursery and reception. When it comes to making the summative assessments for the *end* of nursery and *end* of reception, however, there are significant differences between the two, as the Foundation Stage Profile is only applicable to reception age children. But, as one reception teacher in a school with a nursery class said: *'We are relieved that the Profile takes place at the end of the reception year, as it supports our way of working and continuity across both nursery and reception.'*

Making a termly summary for the Foundation Stage Profile in reception

Having reviewed the record and set appropriate learning priorities or targets, this will be the ideal opportunity for reception teachers to make a summative assessment in line with the Foundation Stage Profile. Based on the evidence collected in the record, which statements have been achieved in which scales? There are likely to be some gaps, for example in a particular scale where no evidence has yet been recorded. But completing the Profile once per term in this way is likely to make the task of completing it at the end of the year much less onerous. At first this may be quite time-consuming until teachers become more familiar with the statements themselves. Whether or not the Profile is completed in this way is up to the team and school to decide, but reviewing the record and feeding the planning points into the planning process is much more important and must not be omitted. The 'official' completion of the Foundation Stage Profile is, of course, at the end of the reception year.

What should happen in nursery?

Schools with nursery classes or foundation stage units will begin their foundation stage records based on observations at the beginning of nursery and carry these through to the end of reception. A smooth-running system will have been created, so long as the records for each child are regularly reviewed and learning priorities highlighted, keeping track of progress and feeding planning to ensure the child's learning is supported. Figure 7.7 shows how this system should work, over a two-year period, involving the children themselves and parents regularly, throughout nursery and reception, but also completing the Foundation Stage Profile termly in reception.

In nursery, too, there is a need for a summative annual report to parents. For children in separate nursery provision and nursery schools, this is also the transfer record to the primary school. Many LEAs provide transition records from nursery to reception which consist of blank boxes for each area of learning, for staff to complete – summarising from the ongoing records, celebrating achievements and individuality and also showing where the child needs further support. This, I believe, is the best approach, respecting and valuing the child's personal achievements, so carefully documented through the observations and other evidence which has been collected.

Other LEAs, commercial companies and teachers have felt the need to create their own tracking system or checklist, usually from Stepping Stones and Early Learning Goals. Personally, I do not like this way of working, because checking a child against a list of predetermined skills is not helpful to teaching, and does not highlight what is significant or celebrate a child's real personal achievements. Where a good system exists, collecting evidence in all areas of learning, as described in Chapter 4, there is no need for a checklist. But I am aware that some feel the need to create one, tracking every child's progress in the same way, rather than in a way which is individual to their own significant progress.

The Foundation Stage Profile is only intended for reception classes (or those children in their final year of the foundation stage). For nursery-age children, the Stepping Stones broadly indicate what is expected, but the Profile has made very limited use of Stepping Stone statements. Even the statements in the Stepping Stones themselves are very limited as they were only designed as a guide to the curriculum, not as an assessment checklist.

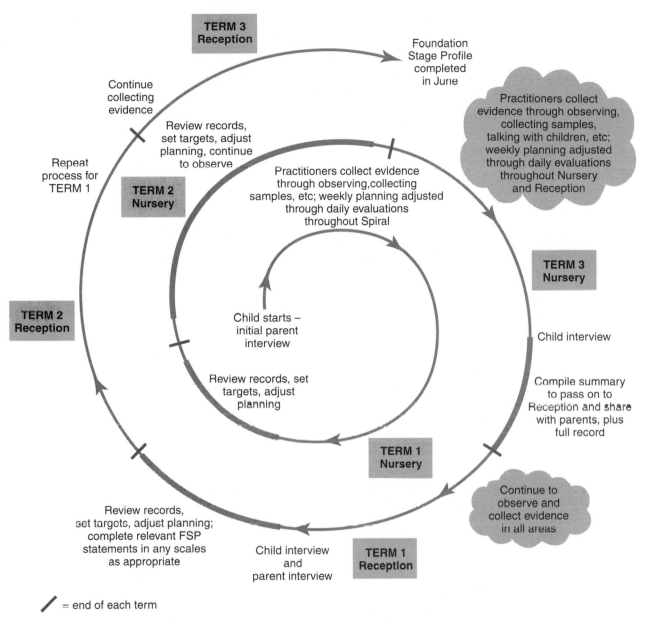

Fig 7.7 The 'assessment for learning' spiral

Learning maps and other tracks

Perhaps the best way forward for those who feel they have to have some kind of tracking device is to do what two of the practitioners in the case studies have done. They created their own system for tracking progress across nursery and reception – a much more comprehensive system than the Stepping Stones, Early Learning Goals and Profile statements. In Chapter 6 Andrea described her 'learning map' and how she created it using her knowledge of child development and other curriculum documents and guides. This is used for long-term planning, but also as a *guide* to assessment.

Lisa too developed her own summative tracking system based on the Stepping Stones and Early Learning Goals to go right across from the beginning of nursery to the end of reception. Her list now includes the Foundation Stage Profile statements, although she devised her approach long before these existed. Each individual stepping stone or goal statement has been separated out and some additional statements added, to show progression in a way that makes better sense. Some of the stepping stone statements have been re-organised under new headings which fit better with child development and are tailored to her own curriculum (for example, the physical section includes 'gymnastics'). All of the foundation stage teachers in her school use this tracking system once per half-term for every child, highlighting statements most applicable to the child.

For example, under *Communication, Language and Literacy – Reading*, there are some significant gaps in the Stepping Stones, which means that if used to assess children, many children will be hovering between the steps for a long time, with little acknowledgement of progress. Some aspects of early literacy development barely appear at all. The result is that the Stepping Stones appear as a linear progression through large leaps, rather than the wonderful maze of pathways which lead children into the complex process of becoming literate. Lisa solved this problem by threading her own statements into the Stepping Stones, turning twelve statements into twenty, but making the whole more holistic. Of course, many more statements could be added too.

Completing the Profile for the final assessments

The Foundation Stage Profile is merely a summative checklist for keeping track of broad progress, which has to be completed at the end of the reception year. As stated before: it does not support teaching or learning! If a system of regular reviews, discussions with parents and conferences with the child has been established, completing the Profile should be relatively easy and not too time-consuming. It is not easy to illustrate this process in full in a book such as this, as it would require the space to include the whole of a child's record! However, what follow are some excerpts and observations, samples, showing how they could lead to making the final judgements in the Profile. Two scales only have been chosen, for two different children.

Fig 7.8 *Rabia's story: typical achievement towards the end of her reception year*

Rabia   Communication for language and for thinking

Rabia's first language is Urdu. When she began in nursery a year before entering the reception class she was at an early stage in learning English.

Statements	Evidence (only some of the evidence is recorded here)	Achieved
1. Listens and responds	All the observations show that R has achieved this	✓
2. Initiates communication with others, displaying greater confidence in more informal contexts	As above, displays confidence in all situations	✓
3. Talks activities through, reflecting on and modifying actions	As above	✓
4. Listens with enjoyment to stories, songs, rhymes and poems, sustains attentive listening and responds with relevant comments, questions or actions	Lots of examples in her reading record show her approach to stories and rhymes, read, told and sung. Able to evaluate verbally too in lots of situations e.g., 20/3 *'I liked the book because it had a little party'*; 22/3 reading The Big Race: related the book to her own experience. Also lots of observations in imaginative play with peers and in investigations, asking questions and commenting.	✓
5. Uses language to imagine and recreate roles and experiences	Too many examples to list, e.g. a scribed story: *Once upon a time there was a queen and she was in her bed. She lived in a castle and she woke up. She heard a noise and went downstairs to check and it was a tiger. It made her jump. He said 'Would you like a ride?' She said 'Yes'. She went on his back and then he stopped. She said 'Go slowly' and she told him to go back home. She went back home, closed the door and went back to bed.*	✓
6. Interacts with others in a variety of contexts, negotiating plans and activities and taking turns in conversation	All the 'focused' observations show her involved in skilful interactions with others, taking turns in conversation, taking lead in recreating roles. E.g. in outside imaginative *play 'I need to dress the table. Thank you, this is going to be nice . . . I'm going to help you . . . put the pots on the table. Yes that's dinner in there.'* When another child asks if she can join in she says *'Yes we're doing a party.'*	✓
7. Uses talk to organise, sequence and clarify thinking, ideas, feelings and events, exploring the meanings and sounds of new words	Lots of examples show her ability to use talk to organise, sequence and clarify thinking. E.g. In garage role play: *'Get me some petrol. That must be the reason the car won't start'*	✓
8. Speaks clearly with confidence and control, showing awareness of the listener	So many examples of this in a variety of group situations including retelling stories to whole class	✓
9. Talks and listens confidently and with control, consistently showing awareness of the listener by including relevant detail. Uses language to work out and clarify ideas, showing control of a range of appropriate vocabulary	Although the above observations show Rabia's confident use of language for communication, storytelling, imaginative play, negotiating and taking the lead in play with others, in self-chosen activities, there are some situations where she is not so confident yet, such as being confident in English to explain her ideas and predictions in more structured activities.	

Oscar   *Knowledge and Understanding of the World*

Statements	Evidence *(only some of the evidence is recorded here)*	Achieved
1. Shows curiosity and interest by exploring surroundings	All the observations show that O has achieved this	✓
2. Observes, selects and manipulates objects and materials. Identifies simple features and significant personal events.	As above, talks about home experiences, events and places, as many observations show!	✓
3. Identifies obvious similarities and differences when exploring and observing. Constructs in a purposeful way, using simple tools and techniques	As above, persists with exploration and constructing. E.g. 15/10 Made a chopstick by rolling paper and sticking with sellotape; planned what he was going to do before hand	✓
4. Investigates places, objects, materials and living things, by using all the senses as appropriate. Identifies some features and talks about those features she/he likes and dislikes	Lots of examples in show his interest in exploring and investigating and hypothesising, for example observing maggots *'may be they slither to move'*. Predicted that if paper was put into the water tray *'It might go soggy'*.	✓
5. Asks questions about why things happen and how things work. Looks closely at similarities, differences, patterns and change	Too many examples to list, e.g. how you know whether something is dead or alive: *'The fish are alive because they're swimming. If they were dead they'd be lying on the top. The shell is dead because it can't move.'*	✓
6. Finds out about past and present events in own life and in those of family members and other people s/he knows. Begins to know about own culture and beliefs and those of other people	In focused observation, he talked a lot to his peers about his family. Joins in all the discussions in circle times about topics to do with cultures and beliefs. Brought in things from home in our international week and talked about them. Talked about his holiday in the Caribbean to see his grandmother. Participated fully in the visit to Chinatown for Chinese New Year, Eid and Diwali celebrations.	✓
7. Finds out about and identifies the uses of everyday technology and uses information and communication technology and programmable toys to support her/his learning	Observations show him able to use Pixie. Predicted it would take 6 moves to get to his friend, pressed button 6 times then pressed go. On computer, repeated the instructions to himself as he used the mouse to drag the items: *'Now drag all the blue things. Hurray!'* Used computer to order numerals correctly	✓
8. Builds and constructs with a wide range of objects, selecting appropriate resources, tools and techniques and adapting her/his work where necessary	Lots of observations of constructions including drawing plans, to show what he intended to make. Focused activity to make a model as long as the piece of paper on the table: made a rocket from boxes, pots and corks. Carefully measured it at each stage to determine which boxes to use then measured precisely the final length.	✓
9. Communicates simple planning for investigations and construction and makes simple records and evaluations of her/his work. Identifies and names key features and properties, sometimes linking different experiences, observations and events. Begins to explore what it means to belong to a variety of groups and communities	Reading back over the collected evidence on Oscar's development in this area of learning, it is clear that he has achieved point 9, (see statement 8, carefully measuring to check lengths). In investigations there are frequent examples of him predicting the outcomes and giving detailed reasons, using a wide descriptive vocabulary appropriately: *'sea lion is sinking because it is heavy, boat floats because it has no holes in it'* and how maggots move *'Maybe they slither'*. Joins in whole class discussions about the local community talking about features he is aware of.	✓

Managing the processes

8

The Foundation Stage Profile has been welcomed by many teachers. Here is a typical comment: *'We are feeling very positive about the Profile, because we are already used to observing children. The Profile supports our formative assessment approach.'*

For others, however, changes to assessment practice will be needed: *'The Foundation Stage Profile has made me realise that we need to move away from our previous methods of assessment in reception. We will need to keep track of what we need to observe and plan times to observe.'*

These different responses to the Profile illustrate how reception class practice has varied from one school to another when it comes to assessment. For those who need to make changes to their assessment processes to meet expectations for the Profile, there may well be other changes to be considered too, such as the organisation of routines and the classroom environment.

Implications for schools and teachers

For an observation-based record-keeping and assessment system to be successfully implemented, well-established foundation stage practice will need to be in place. The Foundation Stage Profile has implications well beyond assessment processes. In this chapter we look particularly at:

- the learning environment for independent learning, inside and outside;
- the styles of teaching and how practitioners support children's learning;
- the organisation of routines;
- the organisation of assessment and planning;
- encouraging links with parents;
- continuity across the foundation stage;
- supporting staff professional development.

A vibrant learning environment for independent learning

Throughout this book I have stressed the importance to learning of indoor and outdoor play, but play will only support children's developing thinking, skills and imagination if it is provided in an interesting and thoughtful way. Children need to spend a large part of their day purposefully involved in meaningful self-chosen learning experiences and play. Practitioners need to be able to support children in their play, getting alongside and working with them; they need to be able to observe and have time for informal conversations. This can only happen if a vibrant, stimulating and rich learning environment inside and outside has been created, in which children are expected to be independent.

So what should the environment look like? The best way is to set up areas of provision which will make sense to the children and to the staff. Many of these will be cross-curricular – for example, the areas for role play, small world play, construction, creative (or designing and making) workshop, sand, water and malleable play. Some areas – such as an investigation and exploration area, a maths area, listening area, writing area, book area and art area – will be more clearly defined by areas of learning.

Creating the outside learning environment

As Angela, the nursery nurse in Chapter 6, said, outdoor play can be the best place to observe children at play, functioning at their highest levels. But for this to be so, it must be a stimulating, thoughtfully prepared area, set up before the start of the day in much the same way as inside. It helps if the outdoor area is set up in areas of provision, to ensure all areas of learning are covered, but of course, outdoor areas allow the space to do things on a larger scale than inside. To carry out observations effectively, the provision must be motivating.

There are many useful guides to creating stimulating environments for the foundation stage: one of the best I know is *A Place to Learn* (2002). The authors point out that:

❛ *It is essential that ALL areas of provision are inviting and stimulating; clearly defined for both adults and children; carefully planned for every day; monitored and evaluated; maintained and replenished; safe; clean and tidy.* **9**

What are the implications for schools and practitioners, if we are to get this working well?

Accessibility of resources and use of space

Resources and equipment need to be accessible to the children – for them to get out *and* put back – with plenty of interesting and relevant things. This means clear labelling (bearing in mind the children's abilities to read), well organised resources, not too little and not too much. It does not mean they have to be expensive, but well thought out with the potential for play, supporting existing interests or encouraging new ones. So much can be done with 'reclaimed materials' for construction, water, sand, creative workshop, art, design and technology, maths and so on.

Storage can be a problem. Many reception classes are very small compared to nursery classes, but this should not prevent areas of provision from being created or resources made accessible. There is no need to have a chair for every child, as the only time children are likely to sit down at the same time is on the carpet. The majority of the tables need to be used in the learning bays and workshops, leaving one for small group work. Removing some of the tables and chairs can make a big difference to the space. Where there is a nursery and reception class in the same school, equipment, resources, storage and space should be shared as much as possible. The next thing is to ensure the children are trained not only to use the environment and the resources, but also to *put things away* when they have finished.

Regular monitoring of the areas, replenishing resources and equipment, setting them up in different ways or introducing new things, is necessary, but this can be done with the children – giving a sense of ownership of the environment and helping them to take responsibility. Displays are an important resource for supporting independent learning too.

Styles of teaching

The REPEY research on effective teaching referred to in Chapter 2 has many implications for how staff see their role in supporting children's learning – in other words, style of teaching. Two major findings from this research are the significance of 'sustained shared thinking' between adult and child in supporting learning, and the effective use of formative assessment. It is only as a result of observing that the input from the teacher can be tailored to the child. Both of these points have implications for 'who does what, when and where'.

In nursery settings it is common for practitioners to share the various teaching roles between them during a session, with one carrying out a focused, adult-led activity and another being involved in children's play and self-initiated activities. The more adults, the more there are to get involved in play inside and outside. Where this is not already the practice, a similar pattern needs to be established in reception when there is more than one member of staff. The teacher and nursery nurse or classroom assistant should swap roles regularly, so that the teacher is sometimes involved in play and self-chosen activities and sometimes leading an activity. In both roles, observing is integral to the role – it goes with the job!

Projects and the Reggio Emilia approach

Several practitioners in the case study schools were deeply influenced by the kindergartens of Reggio Emilia, especially the way projects were organised and the time children were given to develop depth of thinking and doing. So many teachers in England talk about the 'pressure' of the curriculum. It is time for a re-think, and the Reggio approach is a good starting point.

In Reggio Emilia, projects are initiated with the children and then developed over a period of time. The children take the lead in what is investigated and how this is done. This is quite unlike much of the topic work traditionally used in the British school system, which is usually instigated by the practitioners and tends to follow a set programme. This approach is likely to be stimulating to the children if practitioners take on board children's interests and let the topic flow. Sometimes in reception classes there has been an expectation that the teachers will follow the schemes of work for the older children – often following the recommended QCA schemes, for each separate national curriculum subject area – making planning and the curriculum disjointed and disconnected from how young children learn.

Organisation of routines

If observations are to be integral to everyday practice, there are implications for the management of time. Are the sessions planned to maximise children's involvement in what they are doing independently or with staff? Is the time spent on managerial-type tasks and routines kept to a minimum? For example, at the beginning of the day, do children self-register with their name labels, rather than having to sit whilst the teacher calls a register? Can they then go straight to an activity of their own choosing, enabling them to talk to parents, settle any child who needs it, and support children in their free choices? This not only helps to build a closer relationship with parents, involving them more in the class, but also ensures children's time is spent engaged in active learning, rather than waiting for something to happen.

Organisation of assessment and planning

The link between assessment and planning was explained in detail in Chapter 7, but there may be many implications for whole-school policies if the way this is done in the foundation stage differs significantly from the rest of the school's procedures. Some headteachers believe that for continuity across the school, procedures must be the same in every year group. However, the foundation stage is now a legal entity, with different curriculum areas and different teaching methodologies. It therefore needs to be treated differently. Play is an important aspect of the day which cannot be planned in the same way as the daily planning used for older children.

The methods of assessment in nursery and reception are tied into the Foundation Stage Profile and are now taking a lead in implementing assessment *for* learning in the primary school context. It is worth noting that at the time of writing there is a national consultation in Wales to bring into being a Foundation Phase for all children from 3 to 7 years old, modelled very much on the Foundation Stage in England. There have been no statutory tests for 7 year olds in Wales since 2001, and records are based on continuous teacher assessment.

Partnership with parents

Effective links with parents are an expectation of the foundation stage and Foundation Stage Profile. Making sure staff are free to talk at either end of the day will be important for parents who bring and collect their children, and encouraging parents to be involved in class is a common practice in most schools.

However, how are links made with parents, whose children might go to some of the increasing number of wrap-around care facilities on school sites or elsewhere? What about children who make the journey between home and school on the school bus? There are many effective ways that schools have bridged this gap: home-school daily diaries, parent consultations geared to times which suit parents best, encouraging parents to talk about how their children are at home, when they are able to come to meetings. The initial meeting with parents before the child starts can be a good time to talk about how the parents might be able to be involved.

Continuity and coordination across the foundation stage

Continuity in primary schools

Although many primary schools have managed to develop their foundation stage classes into a coordinated whole, this is not always possible, particularly where it would require major building works to link classes. In these situations it is still very important that the foundation stage team finds ways to work together, using similar planning and assessment processes and being prepared to share resources. Sometimes staff have organised occasional class exchanges, so that the whole team has the experience across the foundation stage, without disrupting the continuity of experience for the children.

Continuity across nursery and reception is important. Because the foundation stage is different from the national curriculum, it is very difficult to ensure consistency if staff are frequently moved around different year groups. There is a great deal to take on board in terms of the expectations of the foundation stage, learning how to observe, how to provide a rich play environment and the role of the teacher in play, and working as part of a team. If teachers are to be moved in and out of the foundation stage, this will need to be carefully planned, ensuring proper support and additional training.

Continuity with nursery schools and other early years providers

Where there is no nursery class, links need to be made with other early years providers, to ensure information about the children's learning is passed on. Links with maintained nursery schools are usually very strong and work at lots of different levels, particularly through arranging visits to schools concerned, but there are also often curriculum meetings which teachers attend together. Links with the private and voluntary sector early years providers are increasingly being strengthened, as many of these are also involved in implementing the foundation stage. In most areas there are some joint training sessions and local meetings, and practitioners are encouraged to use similar record-keeping formats.

Supporting staff professional development

When implementing anything new, staff training is an important issue. In various parts of this book, interviews with practitioners have shown how important it has been to ensure the whole staff team is trained in how to observe and make assessments from observations. It is also important that the whole early years team can meet and train together. Increasingly, primary schools are encouraging their early years team to take at least one of the five training days per year to train together.

There are implications for headteachers to arrange the contracts of support staff, particularly in reception, to allow them to be more fully involved in foundation stage meetings, for the benefit of the school and the children. Classroom assistants have much to contribute as professionals – albeit often untrained – not to take over the role of teacher or trained nursery nurse, but as people who work in the class whose opinions and observations on the children are valued.

Moderation for the Foundation Stage Profile

The *Foundation Stage Profile Handbook* explains the procedures which the QCA recommends LEAs to follow for moderation, with advice for headteachers and governors on their responsibilities. The moderation process itself is designed to ensure that the Foundation Stage Profile is implemented in a similar way across the country and between different schools and classes, in the interests of consistency and fairness. Many of the statements in the Profile are broad, general and not designed to be measured accurately – they are summarising developing concepts, skills and dispositions. This is not an exact science. Nevertheless, consistency in what the evidence for any statement might look like, and applying it as consistently as possible, is important. The Handbook gives helpful exemplification for each statement.

What can practitioners do to ensure consistency? Sharing observations during these moderation meetings or in daily evaluation meetings should help all staff to make their assessments more consistent across the team. Regular meetings between practitioners in the same school, specifically to share interpretations of evidence from observations and samples, will be important. One of the recommendations in the Handbook is to compare the evidence for three children – a child achieving at level 9, a child achieving at the early learning goal level (statements 4–8) and a child achieving at the stepping stones level (statements 1–3). This is useful, but practitioners may also decide they want to compare judgements on particular aspects of the Profile, such as children with English as an additional language.

Setting up exchanges between staff in the same school can also help, as mentioned earlier, so that another practitioner's observations on some of the children are included, bringing in another perspective. Meetings between local schools will also help and it may be possible to arrange exchanges of teachers between schools, meeting afterwards to discuss the children.

Taking stock: where have we got to?

9

There is already much good assessment practice in the foundation stage in this country. Some of the assessment processes used in the early years are at the forefront of the best formative assessment practice across our education system. As one teacher said: *'I think this approach should be taken up through the Key Stages because it is about holistic practice, giving the children a chance to reflect on their learning.'*

The practitioners involved in this type of effective formative assessment practice have set up their record-keeping and assessment systems in the way advocated in this book: observing, making assessments from observations, taking note of children's interests and achievements, making links to planning, and involving the child and parents in the process.

As another teacher said: *'Through the processes we use for record-keeping, we feel we can both protect and promote what we consider to be real learning for young children.'*

This good practice shows respect for children and their all-round development, and celebrates their achievements. By using information from assessment to adjust plans, practitioners are able to tailor what is provided to the children's individual needs and interests, and help them to make progress.

The Foundation Stage Profile is merely a summative assessment for the end of the foundation stage and, as such, not too much time or energy should be spent on it. But what it brings with it is a holistic approach to early years assessment, looking *for* and *at* learning in line with child development. As Lesley Staggs, director of the Early Childhood Unit at the DfES, said at a Foundation Stage Profile conference in 2003, the foundation stage is a *'distinct stage of learning with a distinct "what" (the curriculum content) and distinct "how" (promoting appropriate teaching methods to support young children's learning)'*. The Profile is helping to establish this, by promoting methods of assessment which support learning in an appropriate way.

Where the foundation stage itself has been well-established, with appropriately trained early years staff who are experienced at observing and using observations as part of their daily practice, implementing the Foundation Stage Profile will be unproblematic. But there are still questions and concerns about the processes involved, as well as the Profile itself. So here are answers to some of these questions.

Questions about general assessment processes

▶ **How do we find the time to do all this observing, writing up assessments and compiling records?**

Observing, assessing and compiling records should be seen as part of the role of the practitioner to do in the daytime when the children are in the class. If the staff understand how to make assessments from observations, the majority of these can be made at the time the observation is carried out. There is no need to spend time after school doing this. Compiling the records into individual folders with the children provides some very valuable learning, giving them the chance to discuss and reflect on what they have been doing. It also boosts positive dispositions to learning and helps children to understand the processes of learning. The only part of the process which will require additional time away from the classroom is writing up the end-of-year reports and completing the Foundation Stage Profile itself.

However, getting a new system started can be time-consuming at first. There may be a need for some training for the staff team to support those staff less familiar with the processes. This could mean arranging to carry out some paired observations or discussing what to look for when making assessments.

▶ **Our assessments are made using the school's checklist of Stepping Stones and Early Learning Goals rather than observations. Where should we start to make changes?**

Checklists do not support teaching. The foundation stage expects practitioners to make observations, looking for what is significant to the children's learning. As a starting point, begin by getting all the staff team to note down what they observe children do in some of the planned adult-directed activities. This is a good starting point as there will be some expected outcomes to look for. Then once staff have become more confident at these, gradually build in more types of observations, holding regular discussions with the staff team to evaluate the implementation of the new system. Making a tracking sheet to show which children have been observed, and the date, will show the gaps and help to work out who to observe and what kind of observing to do. By the end of a few weeks you will have real evidence of children learning – much more significant to each child than a checklist, and much more informative to the staff team.

▶ **How do we make our observations and ongoing records presentable enough to parents and the children?**

Practitioners are often concerned that their ongoing records are not presentable enough to share. A particular concern is spelling and handwriting. The records are notes staff make whilst working with the children. Parents need to be informed about the purpose of the ongoing records and that writing in a hurry means that they are never perfectly written. Whatever happens, do *not* write them out a second time, in order to make them presentable! Neat writing should only to be reserved for reviews and summaries. The observations should be written in a positive way – highlighting what the child can do and needs help with. If staff are not writing their observations in this way, there is a need for training or discussion.

▶ **How can we feed our ongoing assessments into planning, when we have several classes and we all plan together?**

Planning takes place on several levels: the *short term* (what will be provided for children to do independently as well as the planned adult-led activities); the *medium term* (on a broader level, forward planning usually for a few weeks) and *long term* (an overview of what it is intended for the children to learn over the foundation stage). Short-term planning may be daily or weekly, but it is this which the assessment information needs to feed into. If this is not happening, then planning will not be fine-tuned to the children's learning needs.

The daily evaluation within each class will provide the opportunity to target the discussion to specific children, then adjust plans accordingly. Each class team will need to meet separately to focus the discussion. If the setting is open plan, such as in a Foundation Stage Unit, evaluations will need to be in smaller groups, perhaps dividing by the area of provision a group of staff were working in that day, or into key worker groups.

Questions about the Foundation Stage Profile

► **How will I get time to teach, with all this observing? Am I supposed to have observations for each statement in the Profile?**

Many reception teachers have expressed concern about the Foundation Stage Profile because of the amount of time they feel they are expected to spend observing. There are usually two issues: that it is time taken away from teaching; and that there is too much paperwork.

Both of these are misconceptions of what the Foundation Stage Profile is all about. First, observing is very much at the heart of teaching. Observing is the only way of recording children in the *process* of learning, but most of the observations will be quick notes taken as you work with the children. But samples and photographs, too, provide a great deal of evidence and, when collected over time, are a really good way of showing progress visually.

There will need to be a collection of evidence from observations and samples collected over time before completing the assessments for the Foundation Stage Profile. Most of the Profile statements are broad, and several are repeated in different areas of learning – for example, 'awareness of cultures and beliefs' appear under *Personal, Social and Emotional Development* and also in *Knowledge and Understanding of the World*. Having an observation for every statement would also contravene one of the principles in Chapter 3: it would mean that *a predetermined list of skills, rather than the child,* was the starting point for the record!

So long as the teacher is providing the class with a rich and varied play-based curriculum covering all the aspects of learning, then the scales will be bound to have been covered, and collecting evidence of learning is not an add-on extra: it is just part of what happens as normal classroom practice. One observation of rich, meaningful play will usually provide a great deal of evidence in several different aspects of learning. Keeping track of the evidence you have will help to highlight gaps, either in the breadth of the curriculum, or in evidence about what the child is doing. These can be dealt with in the appropriate way, either adjusting curriculum coverage, or collecting a little more evidence.

▶ **Some of the scale statements have several parts. What should you do if a child has only achieved some of these?**

If it is not completely covered, the statement cannot be ticked, but a comment in the Profile to say what has been achieved will be important. Using the exemplification in the Handbook will help you decide: keeping track of what you know about a child through regular reviews may show you whether it is happening and you haven't seen it, or whether the child has not achieved it.

▶ **We have many different languages in the class and bilingual support for only one of these languages. How do we assess these children fairly?**

This is a difficult issue and it would not be fair if several children at the same stages of learning English were assessed differently because there is support for some languages but not others. Children can be assessed in their first languages throughout each scale except for *Communication, Language and Literacy*, where they can only achieve at the stepping stones level in their first language: any achievement above this relates to English.

Some things can be assessed without the need for spoken language at all, and these can be tracked right through the year in the normal way, as for other children. For the language-based statements, however, planning well in advance what other support can be obtained is important. For example, enlisting the support of parents will be particularly important, if necessary finding interpreters from local community organisations. Sometimes older children in the school can be asked to translate or interpret, but only if they are keen to do so. There is some advice about this issue in the *Foundation Stage Profile Handbook*.

▶ **If the Profile is only for reception, how should we involve nursery staff as 'other contributors'?**

There are lots of ways to ensure that nursery staff become significant 'contributors to the Profile', and the choice needs to suit your situation. First and foremost, a holistic approach to the processes of assessment – setting up a coordinated system between nursery and reception – will be essential.

Some school nursery classes pass the whole record for each child onto the reception class, ensuring that parents are able to discuss the child's progress and development regularly during the child's time in both nursery and reception. Others prefer to make a summary, as there is a requirement to write an annual report to parents anyway, sending the whole ongoing record home to the parents at that point and starting a fresh record in reception. If this is done, a few significant and recent samples should be kept and passed to the new class with the summary. Both systems are perfectly acceptable.

In many LEAs, children transfer into reception classes at two or three points during the year and this means that younger children spend less time in reception. If these younger children are in nursery classes and will spend only one or two terms in reception, it would seem sensible for the nursery staff to complete the Foundation Stage Profile for the first one or two terms. In such cases it will be important to pass on the whole record of evidence to reception as well, so that judgements can be moderated alongside the older children in the class.

And finally . . .

In this book, with the help of many children, their teachers and other practitioners, I have outlined the processes of observing, listening to children and assessing their learning in the foundation stage context. This is at the heart of effective early years practice. I have attempted to clarify the underlying principles to the Foundation Stage Profile and the foundation stage itself, because it is important to know *why* we do what we do.

Perhaps the greatest and most exciting development from the Foundation Stage Profile will be that it will help ensure the implementation of the foundation stage itself in reception classes. This has been difficult for many schools, as it has involved a change in approach, moving away from the national curriculum and more formal practice to a much broader, more holistic curriculum.

I believe that good assessment practice where children are observed and listened to raises practitioner's expectations of all the children. Particularly important in this process is observing children in play. This means taking play *seriously*, just as the children do. It means accepting and delighting in the children's achievements and their interests. Ben's teacher believes in the importance of listening to the children in her class. He is only five years old but has a very clear idea about what is important to him.

Ben   Self-Assessment   18/03/03

---

1. *What do you like doing best?*
   - Travelling and then digging for treasure
   - Once I found a bit of an old Victorian plate, an empty Marmite jar and an old lump of crystal

2. *What do you like playing with?*
   - I like drawing things that no-one else has invented

3. *What do you like best about school?*
   - biscuits and milk
   - the computers ("we haven't even got one I can use at home")

4. *What do you think you are learning when you come to school?*
   - learning lots of things
   - most of the time I spend looking at books and designing at the writing area

5. *What do you think you are really good at doing?*
   - I'm a really good artist
   - Designing and building

6. *What don't you like or do you find hard?*
   - I find it really hard opening doors which are jammed in undiscovered places

7. *Do you have a favourite toy/game/book/story/rhyme/song? (as appropriate)*
   - a book that shows me a picture of something which is worth more than diamonds

---

When I grow up "I'm going to find things which are old and I'm going to sell them for £50,000 each if they're very old and £9 each if they're not so old."

Fig 9.1 *Ben's self-assessment interview*

References

Official Publications

QCA (2000) *The Foundation Stage Training Materials.*
QCA/DfES (2000) *Curriculum Guidance for the Foundation Stage.*
QCA (2003) *The Foundation Stage Profile Handbook and Scale Booklet.*
QCA (2003) *Building the Foundation Stage Profile Training Materials*
(for use with the Foundation Stage Profile video).

Curriculum Guides

A Place to Learn (2002) Lewisham Early Years Advice and Resource
Network, tel: 020 8695 9806; eys.advisers@lewisham.gov.uk
Curriculum Guidelines for babies to five year olds (1999, revised 2000)
London Borough of Islington.
Planning for Progress 2: An Early Years Curriculum Framework (2001)
London Borough of Tower Hamlets Early Years Service and
London Borough of Newham Early Years Unit.
Te Whariki: Early Childhood Curriculum (1996) New Zealand Ministry
of Education, Wellington: Learning Media.

Early Childhood Education, Curriculum and Child Development

Boyd Cadwell, L. (1997) *Bringing Reggio Emilia Home*, Teachers
College Press, Columbia University.
Bruce, T. (1987) *Early Childhood Education,* Hodder and Stoughton.
Clark, A., and Moss, P. (2001) *Listening to Young Children: The Mosiac
Approach*, National Children's Bureau and Joseph Rowntree
Foundation.
Cousins , J. (1999) *Listening to Four Year Olds*, National Early Years
Network.
Gardner, H. (1999) *Intelligence Reframed*, Basic Books.
Goleman, D. (1996) *Emotional Intelligence*, Bloomsbury.
Laevers, F. (2002) *Research on Experiential Education Reader: A selection
of articles by Ferre Laevers,* Centre for Experiential Education,
Leuven.
Paley, V.G. (1990) *The Boy Who would Be a Helicopter: the uses of
storytelling in the classroom,* Harvard University Press.

Pascal, C., Bertram, T. *et al.* (1995, 2003) *Effective Early Learning Programme. Evaluating and Improving Quality in Early Childhood Settings: A Professional Improvement Programme*, University College Worcester.

Siraj-Blatchford, I., Sylva, K., *et al.* (2002) *Researching Effective Pedagogy in the Early Years*, DfES.

Vygotsky, L. (1978) *Mind in Society,* Harvard University Press.

Wood, D. (1998) *How Children Think and Learn,* Blackwell.

Early Years Assessment

Assessment Reform Group (1999) *Assessment for Learning: Beyond the Black Box*, University of Cambridge School of Education.

Assessment Reform Group (2002) *Assessment for Learning: Ten Principles,* www.assessment-reform-group.org.uk

Bertram, T. and Pascal, C. (2002) 'Assessing what matters in early years', in Fisher, J. (Ed.) *Foundations of Learning*, Open University Press.

Black, P. and Wiliam, D. (1998) *Inside the Black Box: Raising Standards through Classroom Assessment*, Kings College, London, Dept of Education and Professional Studies.

Carr, M. (2001) *Assessment in Early Childhood Settings: Learning Stories, Effective Early Learning*, Paul Chapman Publishing.

Gura, P., and Hall, L. (2000) 'Self assessment' in *Early Years Educator*, June 2000, Mark Allen Publishing.

Hutchin, V. (1999) *Right from the Start: Effective Planning and Assessment in the Early Years*, Hodder and Stoughton.

Hutchin, V. (2000) *Tracking Significant Achievement in the Early Years*, 2nd edition, Hodder and Stoughton.

London Borough of Merton (2003) *Assessment and Record-keeping in the Foundation Stage.*

Primary Language Record Handbook (no date), ILEA/Centre for Language in Primary Education.